FOUNDATIONS OF MODERN POLITICAL SCIENCE SERIES
Robert A. Dahl, Editor

The
Policy-Making
Process

FOUNDATIONS OF MODERN POLITICAL SCIENCE SERIES

ENGLEWOOD CLIFFS, NEW JERSEY Prentice-Hall, Inc.

CHARLES E. LINDBLOM

Yale University

To Susan, Steven, and Eric

ACKNOWLEDGMENTS. For their invaluable criticism and suggestions, my thanks to Professors J. D. Barber, R. A. Dahl, D. J. Danelski, J. W. Fesler, F. I. Greenstein, and D. W. Rae, each of whom read part or all of a draft of the manuscript.

FOUNDATIONS OF MODERN POLITICAL SCIENCE SERIES

Robert A. Dahl, Editor

C

74806

Contents

v

Contents

Policy Making and Political Science

Social scientists have to guard against a tendency
to explain things that are already fairly well known.
Most people—even poets and ballet dancers—know a good deal about policy
making. They know, for example, that the immediate responsibility for
policy making has to be delegated to officials, that interest-group
and party leaders greatly influence these officials, and that
the rest of us play less active (though not insignificant) roles
in the policy-making drama. Yet many aspects of policy
making still need explaining, because almost no one

is well satisfied with his understanding of how policy is made. All kinds of further questions spring to mind. They are the subject of this book. Some of them are:

Questions on the underlying processes by which policy is made:

What are the major sources of power in policy making?

Do ordinary citizens significantly influence the specific policy choices of government?

Are constitutional and other legal rules effective in assigning policy-making responsibilities to various officials, or is there a set of informal rules that counts for more?

Questions on the intelligence of the policy-making process:

To what extent do information and analysis really count in the making of policy? Are they only window-dressing?

How could we have gotten into such a fiasco as the Bay of Pigs episode?

Questions on democracy in policy making:

To what extent, if at all, is the growing technical complexity of government tasks, as in space exploration, transferring the job of policy making from politician to technician?

Is there an Establishment? Does it make policy?

Questions on possible institutional rigidities and irrationalities:

Why do we go on and on, decade after decade, dealing with so many of the same problems—farm prices, strikes, old-age insurance, and care of the mentally infirm, for example? Why do we fail to solve these problems?

Does it matter much which party wins an election? In the dispute over Vietnam, why hawks and doves in each party instead of hawks in one, doves in the other?

Who *really* makes policy on an issue, like tariffs, that greatly affects economic life? Congress and President? Wall Street? General Motors?

Questions on alternative policy-making systems:

Is it true that policy in Britain is more responsive to the majority, and in the U.S. more responsive to minorities?

Could we in the U.S. more effectively stimulate economic growth if we had a planning commission on, say, the French model?

Is there any sense in the common American practice of splitting up policy-making responsibility among competing policy makers in a single field—for example, setting the U.S. Treasury Department and the Federal Reserve Board in conflict with each other for the control of monetary policy?

The policy-making process is not one of the standard fields of political science, as are comparative government, international relations, or the history of political thought. Nor does it appear on a list of traditional inquiries into politics, like the origins of the state, the conditions of viability of a political system, the rationale for democracy, or the ideal political system. Nevertheless, it now reflects a converging curiosity, on the part of social scientists,

2

Policy Making and Political Science

philosophers, mathematicians, and psychologists, about decision-making processes.[1]

Psychologists ask: How does man use his mind to solve problems? Economists ask: How does he choose among alternatives so as to get the most of what he wants? Philosophers ask: How does he decide on what is valuable? Students of public administration ask: How do men make an organization serve their purposes? Political scientists believe that all these questions, and some others as well, ought to be asked about *political* decisions. And mathematicians offer various formal techniques to give these questions a precise formulation and to help answer them.

To be sure, political philosophers and political scientists have always studied how policies are and ought to be made; but their concern has usually been subordinated to the traditional topics or, as often has occurred in recent years, to the study of how conflicting interests are reconciled in a society.[2] Aspects of the policy-making process have also been studied in specific inquiries into the legislative, executive, and judicial processes and into party and interest-group politics.[3]

The idea of making "the policy-making process" itself a major focus for specialized inquiry is still so new that no one seems to want to answer the question of what is supposed to be included in the process and what excluded from it. The usefulness of the concept is even implicitly called into question by many political scientists who now come close to defining politics as a whole as a policy-making process.[4] For if "the policy-making process" refers to politics as a whole, it is not a concept that directs us to any particular phase or aspect of political phenomena.

The Policy-Making Focus

Nevertheless, we are going to use the concept of the policy-making process to achieve a focus of inquiry into certain aspects of political processes. What specifically will distinguish this focus, or way of looking at political phenomena, from others? For the most part, we will demonstrate it, not talk about it. But one characteristic of policy making important for our method is worth noting here and now: its complexity and apparent disorder.

[1] For a survey of the work done in these disciplines, see D. W. Taylor, "Decision Making and Problem Solving" in J. G. March, *Handbook of Organizations* (Chicago: Rand McNally & Co., 1965).

[2] For example, D. B. Truman, *The Governmental Process* (New York: Alfred A. Knopf, 1951).

[3] A representative set of examples: J. C. Wahlke, H. Eulau, W. Buchanan, and L. C. Ferguson, *The Legislative System* (New York: John Wiley and Sons, Inc., 1962); D. Lockard, *The Politics of State and Local Government* (New York: The Macmillan Company, 1963); S. H. Beer, *British Politics in the Collectivist Age* (New York: Alfred A. Knopf, 1966); and R. E. Neustadt, *Presidential Power* (New York: John Wiley and Sons, Inc., 1960).

[4] See, for example, how close the following two definitions of politics come to identifying politics with the policy-making process: "Politics is the activity . . . by which an issue is agitated or settled" (M. Meyerson and E. C. Banfield, *Politics, Planning and the Public Interest* [Glencoe, Ill.: The Free Press, 1955], p. 304); and ". . . politics consists of struggle among actors pursuing conflicting desires on public issues" (V. Van Dyke, "The Optimum Scope of Political Science," in J. C. Charlesworth (ed.), *A Design for Political Science: Scope, Objectives, and Methods* [Philadelphia American Academy of Political and Social Science, 1966], p. 2).

One is tempted to think that policy is made through a sequence of steps (or a set of interlocked moves), such as: (a) preliminary appraisal of or inquiry into the problem; (b) identification of goals or objectives; (c) canvassing of possible policies to achieve the goals; and, (d) choice or decision.[5] This way of looking at policy making is useful for some purposes, but it tends to view policy making as though it were the product of one governing mind, which is clearly not the case. It fails to evoke or suggest the distinctively political aspects of policy making, its apparent disorder, and the consequent strikingly different ways in which policies emerge.

A policy is sometimes the outcome of a political compromise among policy makers, none of whom had in mind quite the problem to which the agreed policy is the solution. Sometimes policies spring from new opportunities, not from "problems" at all. And sometimes policies are not decided upon but nevertheless "happen." No one would say that the British government of India planned mass starvation in Bengal during World War II. Yet government did not bring adequate grain into the famine area, as it could have. In an important sense, then, tolerating starvation in Bengal was established as a government policy, without anyone's explicitly deciding on it.

We are going to look at policy making as an extremely complex analytical and political process to which there is no beginning or end, and the boundaries of which are most uncertain. Somehow a complex set of forces that we call "policy making," all taken together, produces effects called "policies." We want to learn what we can about the network of causes of these effects.

LIMITS OF THE ANALYSIS

Wealthy nations spend more of national income on science and education than do poor nations, and more on highways and on traffic control. And, two governments with strikingly different policy-making systems—one democratic, the other authoritarian—may follow similar policies with respect to money and credit, industrial development, or education because the two are alike in wealth, complexity of economic and social structure, and technology.[6] Clearly, then, policy is molded by a variety of forces beyond those within the policy-making system itself. Our analysis of policy making will not do justice to them all. In this one short book, we will do well to achieve a clear outline of the system itself.

[5] Harold Lasswell's well-known set consists of intelligence and planning, recommending, prescribing, invoking, applying, appraising, terminating. Among other places, it is presented in Lasswell, "The Public Interest," in C. J. Friedrich (ed.), *The Public Interest* (*Nomos,* Vol. 5), (New York: Atherton Press, 1962).

[6] For a summary of some earlier studies and for some new investigations into economic determinants of government policies, see T. R. Dye, *Politics, Economics, and the Public* (Chicago: Rand McNally & Co., 1966).

Policy Making and Political Science

Policy
Analysis

C H A P T E R   T W O

At one time or another almost everyone complains about "politics"
in policy making. We like neither selfish partisanship nor outright
incompetence. In the United States most of us see little justification
for: pork-barreling in public constructions projects; undermanning
our courts and piling up untried cases; failing to curb mugging in city
parks and streets; giving tax concessions, tariff protection,
and other favors to interests powerful enough to win them; awarding
contracts to friends of the aldermen or mayor; encouraging riots
by perpetuating slums and discrimination.

5

We suspect that "politics" accounts for such apparent irrationalities as:

India's irresolution on population control
England's failure to stimulate more rapid economic growth
The Soviet Union's long record of weakness in agricultural development

Examples like these pose a double-barreled question: Can policy making be analytic and scientific, or does "politics" always dominate? How far can analysis go in policy making?

The fact is that it already goes further than many people think. In all governments all over the world, a standard routine for reaching a policy decision is to gather and analyze facts, doing so with at least implicit theory. If analysis is often hurried and sometimes superficial, it is never wholly absent; and we need to appreciate its scope before we lament that it seems to be pushed aside by "politics." Let us look at some indications of its scope.

Routine Analysis

AN EXAMPLE FROM FOREIGN POLICY

Consider the annual U. S. policy decision concerning the level of foreign aid to Pakistan. In the Pakistan Mission of the Agency for International Development (AID), throughout the year various staff members carry on a running scrutiny of Pakistan's use of previous aid. They also carry on a discussion, orally and through an exchange of papers, on what objectives the U. S. should seek in the Pakistan aid program. For its analyses, the Mission taps a variety of skills: of engineers, economists, administrators, lawyers, and persons with assignments in specific fields like technical assistance, capital development, agricultural methods, credit, minerals and mines. Some officers in Pakistan design the "country program" and send it for amendment to AID in Washington.

The Washington office rolls up a battery of analytic artillery. In addition to its own internal studies, it draws on special analyses such as those undertaken by the Clay Committee on AID policy which was appointed by President Kennedy. Washington staff members consult other departments and agencies, like the Bureau of the Budget, the Department of Defense, and the Treasury Department. Staff members from these various departments and agencies gather for group discussion and for debate on position papers. They assemble not merely to invoke their authority over each other; they thrash out the merits of various possible policies on aid level to Pakistan.

AN EXAMPLE FROM AMERICAN STATE POLITICS

Several years ago a governor wanted to develop a program of subsidized public housing for low-income groups in his state. He called on the staff of the state public housing authority, as well as on his own executive staff and members of a nearby university faculty, for analysis. For what income group

6

should the housing program be designed? About how many housing units should be authorized? How could funds be raised? As he knew, it would be impossible to come to any specific conclusion on policy without further analysis of these questions.

Each of these questions in turn spawned others. How many people were in the market for low-cost housing? Was enough construction labor available for a big program? Could building codes be simplified to permit new methods that would lower cost and hence expand the possible market? Should housing be financed by short-term or by long-term borrowing? Since short-term borrowing would be relatively more advantageous if the future course of the interest rate were downward, and long-term borrowing would be relatively advantageous if it were upward, the investigators were pushed on into such questions as probable interest-rate movements over the next decades.

The investigators also looked into the relative merits of subsidizing home ownership and subsidizing rental units, and this question led them into an examination of the reductions in housing costs that might be achieved for a subsidized family by do-it-yourself home maintenance—more feasible for an owner than for a renter. All these questions were studied by the governor and his staff, even if the final resolution of some of them was later caught up in "political" maneuvering.

AN EXAMPLE FROM ABROAD

Even in a country in which a low national income and a scarcity of technical skills make analysis relatively difficult, the role of analytic policy making is not to be underestimated. India, for example, has been wrestling for a number of years with policy on irrigation. In general, Indian policy has been to distribute water thinly. Millions of Indian farmers therefore receive water supplies helpful for forestalling drought in dry years even if it is insufficient to achieve a steady annual increase in yields. One of several high-level policy questions now before the government of India is: Should policy move away from distribution of thin water supplies for drought relief and toward concentration of water supplies in smaller areas for sustained high yields?

Because the question reveals an outright conflict between the many and the few (a little water for many or more water for a few), it might be thought that the solution simply depends on where the power lies—with the many or with a possibly privileged few. In fact, however, the Ministry of Irrigation and Power, the Ministry of Food and Agriculture, and the Planning Commission, together with the corresponding agencies in the various states, as well as the Ford Foundation in India, the Rockefeller Foundation, the U. S. Aid Mission, the World Bank, and various university faculties and research groups in India like the Institute for Economic Growth, are engaged in studies bearing on the question. In any one year, documents produced by these various agencies that bear directly on this policy question run into the many hundreds of pages. They grapple with such analytical questions as: What is the input-output relationship for various crops in various areas as the available water per acre is increased? Is it cheaper to get output increases by bringing water to new areas or by increasing the water supply to already irrigated areas? On what grounds can one justify concentrating the benefits of

7

irrigation on relatively few farmers rather than dispersing these benefits over many?[1]

Specialized Institutions and Processes for Policy Analysis

To judge the scope of analytic policy making, however, we need more than these examples; we need also to sample quickly the number and variety of specialized government procedures for analysis. Almost everyone is familiar with such devices as the legislative investigative committee and the "big-name" commission, the latter incorporating prominent private citizens appointed by prime ministers, presidents, governors, mayors, department heads, or other officials or agencies. Their studies are sometimes ambitious; the two Hoover Commissions on governmental reorganization, for example, each enlisted several hundred prominent citizens as members of committees and task forces, together with hundreds of paid professional staff.

An illustration of a device compelling comprehensive systematic analysis of proposed policies and their costs is central budgeting, as in the U. S. Bureau of the Budget and in comparable organizations in the states and in the finance ministries of other countries. Budgeting has outlived its days as an unexciting administrative tool; it has blossomed into a high-level process for systematically appraising policy choices themselves. There are also specialized techniques for focusing on specific problems, such as cost-effectiveness analysis, a set of procedures for quantifying and aggregating the costs and benefits of certain kinds of public expenditures—usually, large public construction projects.

Two similar devices for policy analysis are research grant and research contract, through which a policy-making agency enlists in a systematic way the analytical skills of non-governmental organizations, including consulting firms, research institutes, and universities. U. S. government support of social research through these devices totaled, by one estimate, about $240 million in 1967, and is growing rapidly.[2] Through these devices government not only attacks current policy problems but anticipates future problems. For example, the U. S. National Aeronautics and Space Administration has supported research on such topics as "Economic and International Policy Questions Associated with Communication Satellites."

The Department of Defense or departments within it have used contracts to establish and support non-profit research organizations that work exclusively or largely for them—the RAND Corporation, the Special Operations Research Office, the Human Relations Research Office, the Institute for Defense Analyses, the Institute for Naval Analysis, and the Operations

---

[1] For a final abbreviated example of policy analysis: "The years 1924–28 witnessed a remarkable debate in the Soviet Union. Its major participants were leading Communist theoreticians and eminent non-party economists; the keenly interested audience included everyone who was politically and intellectually articulate in Soviet society. The debate ranged far and wide from issues concerning the theory of value to day-to-day political minutiae." A. Erlich, *The Soviet Industrialization Debate, 1924–28* (Cambridge: Harvard University Press, 1960), p. xv.

[2] U. S., 90th Congress, 1st Session, House of Representatives, Research and Technical Programs Subcommittee of the Committee on Government Operations, *The Use of Social Research in Federal Domestic Programs* (April, 1967), Part I, pp. 22f.

Research Office. Not all of the work of these organizations is policy minded, but much of it is.

The growth of a family of interrelated analytical methods, used primarily in the Department of Defense, illustrates how analytical techniques continue to develop. The first member of the family was operations research. "Operations research" is a name given to a still growing collection of techniques for formally appraising the relative merits of alternative policies, in which every effort is made to quantify the advantages and disadvantages of each alternative and, through probability calculations, to adjust these quantitative estimates to take account of their relative degrees of certainty or uncertainty.

In the application of operations research it became clear, not surprisingly, that in measuring the disadvantages or cost of alternative policies, it would sometimes turn out that disadvantages or costs for one or all alternatives were so high as to throw doubt on the wisdom of the original objective. Operations research was thereupon extended, under the new "systems analysis," to formal analysis of objectives as well as to means to their attainment.

Even with these extensions of analytic policy making in the Defense Department, there remained a discrepancy between military policy making, for which operations research and systems analysis were enlisted, and military budgeting, which these devices had not touched. A key man in the introduction of the new analytical techniques, the then Assistant Secretary (Controller) in the Department of Defense, described the discrepancy: "Planning was performed in terms of missions, weapons systems, and military units or forces. . . ." These are the *outputs* of the Defense Department. But ". . . budgeting, on the other hand, was done in terms of such 'inputs' or intermediate products as personnel, operation and maintenance, procurement, construction, etc. . . ."[3] For making policy, some kind of machinery had to be devised for translating one into the other. This set of techniques for calculating the "input" costs of governmental "outputs" is known as Planning-Programming-Budgeting or, for short, PPB. In 1965, President Johnson began the process of introducing PPB into all departments of government.

Planning represents a new interest among policy makers in *analyzing the interrelations of policies.* A town planning and zoning commission tries to analyze policies pertaining to land use. The U. S. President's Council of Economic Advisers gives some kind of coordination to public policies bearing on employment, the price level, the balance of payments, and economic growth. In Britain, the establishment in 1962 of the National Economic Development Council, like the earlier French *Commisariat du Plan,* permits government to achieve a more informed coordination of price, investment, employment, and foreign trade policies with each other. Even in the less developed countries, planning commissions have been almost everywhere established. With hundreds of staff members, the Indian Planning Commission, for example, is in a position both to bombard Indian policy makers with

[3] C. J. Hitch, *Decision Making For Defense* (Berkeley: University of California Press, 1965), p. 26.

9

considered recommendations in almost any policy field, and to advise on the coordination of development policies generally.

In the Soviet Union, economic planning is an attempt comprehensively to replace the "irrational" forces of the market with rational calculation. It requires a mammoth analytic effort, and a sophisticated one, if the job is to be done well. The Soviets have therefore, for example, explored the possibilities of applying the formal techniques of input-output analysis, originally developed by Leontieff at Harvard University, as well as techniques of mathematical programming of resource allocation.

Non-governmental Resources

In a wealthy and free country like the United States, policy analysis comes to be a massive process engaging millions of citizens and groups. Private corporations, interest groups, universities, and research institutions turn out a vast flow of policy studies and advice to government. Even unaffiliated persons play an important part in analytic policy making: for example, Ralph Nader's *Unsafe at Any Speed* on auto safety policy. And beyond explicit policy analysis, there is a deep and wide river of information, fed by many springs—from formal research projects to modest letters to the *New York Times*—into which policy makers dip for their purposes.[4] For the historic new policy on school desegregation announced in *Brown v. the Board of Education,* for example, the Supreme Court drew on the sociology of race relations—on studies never designed for policy guidance but nevertheless part of an enormous capital fund of knowledge on which explicit policy analysis can at any time draw.

What is possible in policy making in one country may be impossible in another. For countries differ greatly, of course, in their non-governmental resources for analytic policy making: in the number of their highly trained citizens, in the availability of newspapers and other media for dissemination of information, in the number and quality of research institutes, and so on. As an example of the range of difference, Ghana graduates in any one year one college student for every 72,000 persons in the population; the U. S. graduates one for every 400.[5] Some other ratios are:

Turkey	1:6,500
United Kingdom	1:1,800
India	1:1,000
Soviet Union	1: 700

Does Analysis Really Count?

Unquestionably, the analytical input into policy making is great. But one possible reaction to the evidence is dismay. With all this dependence on analysis, why is policy as poor as it is? If policy is so carefully studied, why is it often ill considered, irrational, and distorted by group interest rather than tailored to the public interest? We shall return to this question.

[4] See, for a survey, F. Machlup, *The Production and Distribution of Knowledge in the United States* (Princeton: Princeton University Press, 1962).

[5] UNESCO, *Basic Facts and Figures* (1960), Table 10 and Appendix A.

Another possible reaction to the evidence is outright skepticism. Some will wonder if the analysis of policy is not mere window-dressing. Does analysis really count? Practical policy makers seem to think so. In 1966, on the fiftieth anniversary of the Brookings Institution, a leading policy-oriented research institution, President Johnson said:

Yet in field after field, reports and studies that emerged from Brookings did bring about substantial changes in law and in practice. It was often a case of concentrated brain power applied to national problems where ignorance, confusion, vested interests, or apathy had ruled before. Sometimes the Brookings study won the day; sometimes it only opened the way for other ideas and policies; but always it changed the temperature in the cosmos of Washington.[6]

A recent Budget Bureau Director admonishes:

The cynical view of the matter is that rational calculation in government programming is a harmless but ineffectual pursuit, since all important questions are ultimately decided on "political" grounds. . . . The thesis is wrong if it is taken to mean the findings of skilled and objective analysis of public programs are not influential in decision-making at the highest level. In fact, such findings are usually influential and, not infrequently, decisive.[7]

In our earlier examples, one can hardly doubt the practical significance of analytic policy making for the U. S. aid level to Pakistan, for a state public housing program, for irrigation policies in India. In each of these cases, we saw, it was the policy makers themselves who demanded the policy analysis; it was not thrust on them. Nor can one doubt the evidence that through his *The Other America*, Michael Harrington greatly influenced the development of the present federal anti-poverty program. Or that medical research is necessary to pure-food-and-drug policy; cancer research to policy on cigarette labeling and advertising; economic analysis to policy on taxes, public spending, and money and banking; or analysis of air pollution to bomb-testing policy.

[6] U. S., *The Use of Social Research in Federal Domestic Programs*, Part I, p. 178.

[7] *Ibid.*, p. 2.

Limits on Policy Analysis

All of us at least dimly perceive that analysis is often,
perhaps always, inconclusive; it does not wholly settle a policy
question at issue. Or it goes astray, as in predicting that
bombing would cripple Germany in World War II. Or some participants
in the policy-making process are hostile to analysis;
like prohibitionists, they know what they want and accept
no advice. What then are the limits of policy
analysis? How far can we go in reasoning out policy
instead of fighting over it?

A good way to find out is to specify what a man has to do to analyze a problem rationally, and see where he runs into difficulties. A "classical" formulation runs something like this:

1. Faced with a given problem,
2. a rational man first clarifies his goals, values, or objectives, and then ranks or otherwise organizes them in his mind;
3. he then lists all important possible ways of—policies for—achieving his goals
4. and investigates all the important consequences that would follow from each of the alternative policies,
5. at which point he is in a position to compare consequences of each policy with goals
6. and so choose the policy with consequences most closely matching his goals.

Some people *define* a rational choice as one that meets these conditions. Others have merely claimed that these are the steps that any rational problem-solver should take. Either way, these steps constitute a classical model of rational decision.[1] Let us examine them carefully.[2]

Defining the Policy Problem

Policy makers are not faced with a *given* problem. Instead they have to identify and formulate their problem. Rioting breaks out in dozens of American cities. What is the problem? Maintaining law and order? Racial discrimination? Impatience of the Negroes with the pace of reform now that reform has gone far enough to give them hope? Incipient revolution? Black power? Low income? Lawlessness at the fringe of an otherwise relatively peaceful reform movement? Urban disorganization? Alienation?

To all these formulations, you may reply: The concrete observable problem is the riot itself. But perhaps the riots are merely symptomatic of "real" problems to be solved. Then, the question arises again: What is the "real" problem? During the summer riots of 1967, President Johnson appointed a commission not to solve the problem but first to find out what it was.

Even familiar problems require formulation. A problem like inequality in income distribution can be formulated as one big problem or as many relatively independent smaller problems such as:

inadequate education for the children of low- and middle-income families, for whom we have developed free public education;

[1] For a similar formulation and brief critique of this "classical" model, see H. A. Simon and J. G. March, *Organizations* (New York: John Wiley and Sons, Inc., 1958), pp. 136*ff*. For an elementary survey of contemporary formal decision theory, see D. W. Miller and M. K. Starr, *The Structure of Human Decisions* (Englewood Cliffs, N. J.: Prentice-Hall, Inc., 1967).

[2] We shall follow the critique of the "classical" model developed in D. Braybrooke and C. E. Lindblom, *A Strategy of Decision* (New York: The Free Press, 1963), Part I.

inadequate retirement income, for which we have developed old-age assistance and insurance;

inadequate income for broken families, for whom we have developed aid to dependent children and special benefits through social insurance;

low earnings of the unskilled, for whom we have developed occupational training.

Moreover, there is a large class of problems that needs to be invented when new means or opportunities make new goals possible. Landing a man on the moon never used to be a problem for the U. S. We made it a problem when we began to develop a technology for space exploration that made such a problem possible. A problem is often a new opportunity, not an old sore.

For all these reasons, there is all kinds of room for controversy over what "the problem" is, and no way to settle the controversy by analysis. Here already, then, is a limit on analytic policy making, and a necessary point of entry for "politics" and other "irrationalities" in policy making.[3]

Complexity and Inadequate Information

It is also generally recognized that not one of the above steps 2 through 6 in "classical" problem-solving can actually be completed for complex problems, even with the help of new techniques and electronic computation. A wise policy maker will not even try for completion. To clarify and organize all relevant values, to take an inventory of all important possible policy alternatives, to track down the endless possible consequences of each possible alternative, then to match the multifold consequences of each with the statement of goals—all this runs beyond the capacity of the human mind, beyond the time and energy that a decision maker can afford to devote to problem solving, and in fact beyond the information that he has available. A policy maker, whether an individual or an organization, will become exhausted long before the analysis is exhausted. Hence for complex policy problems, analysis can never be finished; it will always therefore fail to prove that the right policy has been found and will always be subject to challenge. And since it is inconclusive, men will have to fight over the issues remaining to be settled.

Because in Pakistan, as well as in most of the other underdeveloped countries to which we offer aid, the U. S. is engaged in no less ambitious a program than assisting the transformation of an entire society, it cannot possibly complete an analysis of required policy. Even if in the U. S. we see no alternative but to assist such an effort, we still do not *know* how to effect such a transformation. Although we are trying to achieve such a transformation in many places in the world, we have never yet achieved one. We make only an informed guess that economic improvement, toward which we can make concrete contributions, is a means to the desired transformation. We believe, but we do not know, that American participation in the solution of Pakistan's problems will not undercut Pakistan's own energies. As for the

[3] For a detailed analysis of difficulties of defining a policy problem when "there is no consensus on a definition of the problem," see J. W. Fesler, "National Water Resources Administration," in S. C. Smith and E. N. Castle (eds.), *Economics and Public Policy in Water Resource Development* (Ames, Iowa: Iowa State University Press, 1964).

14

magnitude of our assistance, we do not know any way to analyze with any conclusive result such a straightforward question as whether an aid level, say, four times the present level, would or would not better accomplish Pakistan's transformation.

To be sure, analysis can clarify these issues to a point, and even educated guesses are much to be prized in policy making. For such a policy problem, however, analysis remains forever unfinished, and may also run into error.

Time limits. Moreover, even if it were possible for men to gather and organize enough information to solve conclusively a complex problem, in actual political life they will often be asked for a decision long before an analysis can be completed. The U. S. could not have settled down to a conclusive analysis of the merits of defending South Korea when it was invaded.[4] Nor can the Soviets patiently wait for the construction of a table of input-output coefficients before they settle on next year's production policies. Nor did Nasser have time for a serene analysis of the Egyptian bureaucracy's capacity to administer the Suez Canal just before he took control of it from Britain.

Costliness of analysis. It would be easy to spend half a million dollars to explore the effects on business profitability, on shoppers' convenience, and on efficient traffic flows, of making automobile traffic on Church Street in New Haven flow exclusively south instead of north (or of reopening the street to two-way traffic). But no one but an eccentric could think the possible improvement would be worth the cost of the analysis. To be sure, some analysis was undertaken before reaching the decision that now routes all cars north, but analysis had to be supplemented by other forms of decision making, including guessing. On every hand, we can find examples of complexities for which conclusive analysis, if it were possible, would not be worth the cost.

Difficulties in Organizing Goals or Values

Another conspicuous difficulty in analysis is finding appropriate values to guide policy choices; disagreement is inevitable. In the Pakistan case, again, AID officials in Washington will not wholly accept any analyses sent in from the Pakistan Mission, since they know that the on-the-spot involvement of Americans in Pakistan often tends to pull their sympathies toward Pakistan. (Conversely, the Mission rejects to a degree the analysis of the Washington officials, whom they believe undervalue Pakistan.) Similarly, the President, who has the responsibility for achieving all kinds of policy objectives, fears that AID as a whole over-values foreign aid. And AID and the Bureau of the Budget distrust each other, the one because of preoccupation with economic growth, and the other due to preoccupation with economy in the expenditure of public funds. In short, each important participant in policy making on the aid level to Pakistan will assume that analyses undertaken by other participants can at best show how to achieve values significantly different from those he himself wishes to achieve.

[4] On how a quick decision was actually made, see R. C. Snyder and G. D. Paige, "The United States Decision to Resist Aggression in Korea: The Application of an Analytical Scheme," 3 *Administrative Science Quarterly* (December, 1958), pp. 376ff.   15

Let us try to get at the root of the trouble, for the problem is not only disagreement on values, but the difficulties any one analyst has with his own values. Contemporary social science draws a sharp distinction between fact and value. Values cannot be empirically tested. Analysis can therefore neither verify any one person's values nor command agreement among persons on their values.

To be sure, many evaluative statements can be interpreted as empirical propositions and can thus be objectively tested. These are statements intended to be taken as true or false in the light of some accepted criteria. Take for instance the statement, "Everyone should have a good job." If I defend this statement simply by declaring that it formulates one of my ultimate values, then, according to the canons of contemporary social science, the statement cannot be objectively verified. I may, however, be appealing to another value. I may believe, for example, that everyone should have a good job because everyone ought to be well fed and housed. If so, the statement can then be interpreted to mean that people with good jobs will in fact be well fed and well housed. Whether that is true or false can be empirically tested.

Similarly, one can, under some circumstances, test the proposition that everyone ought to be well fed and well housed. Again, if proposed as a declaration of ultimate value, it is not empirically verifiable. But if it is defended by reference to some further proposition such as that everyone should be happy, then the proposition that everyone should be well fed and housed is equivalent to the proposition: "People who are well fed and housed will be happy." This is an empirical proposition in form, hence in principle empirically verifiable.

As we move on and on through such chains or linkages, however, we will increasingly run into woozy abstractions like "happiness" that make empirical propositions containing them impossible to confirm in practice, even though in principle they are verifiable. And in any case, one eventually arrives at the end of the line, whereat some final evaluative propositions, because they cannot be examined in the light of still some further linked proposition, are impossible to verify empirically even in principle. The dominant view in contemporary social science is that these end-of-the-line propositions are impossible to verify both in principle *and* practice. Such propositions have to be simply postulated, taken as axioms, or declared by one who uses them to express his wants, or at least what he wants to recommend to others. Since no empirical proof of any of them is possible, analysis will neither verify them for any one analysis, or bring various analysts into agreement on them.[5]

The older view—taken by Plato, for example—is that the truth of these end-of-the-line propositions is discoverable by a kind of "empirical" observation of the nature of man and universe. But no one has yet discovered all of them, nor have competing would-be discoverers (philosophers) agreed on them. So as a practical matter, any one policy analyst may be uncertain, and

[5] For a survey and analysis of this and competing views on the problem of verifying values, see A. Brecht, *Political Theory* (Princeton: Princeton University Press, 1959).

Limits on Policy Analysis

any group will disagree. Their analyses will consequently remain inconclusive and disputed.[6]

THE POSSIBILITY OF AGREEMENT ON CRITERIA FOR POLICY

But even if end-of-the-line values cannot be objectively verified, might not everyone nevertheless agree on a sufficient number of them so that policy analysts can be guided by them? Do we not all agree, for example, on the value of human life, of freedom, of progress, of reduction of pain, of honesty, and of self-expression? The fact is that the Nazis did not, and many policy makers in communist systems do not. Nor do all Americans accept these values for Negroes. Moreover, even those of us who generally endorse them make important exceptions to some or all of them. We sanction the taking of life in some circumstances, at least as a matter of practical policy. Or we sanction the dishonesty that is essential to political bargaining and negotiation, including negotiation between nations. And we disagree on the exceptions.

In any case, a policy analyst has to descend from a high level of abstraction-like freedom to lower-level values like elimination of capital punishment, equality of educational opportunity, coexistence with the U.S.S.R., or full employment. At this level clearly we do not all agree; and, as a further complication for any one person, values at this level are very much in conflict with each other. Some values have to be sacrificed to achieve others, as when we sacrifice some possibilities for employment by holding down inflation, or suffer some inflation in order to achieve fuller employment.

THE PUBLIC-INTEREST CRITERION

Does the concept of the public interest provide an agreed criteria for policy analysis? Clearly, there is no general agreement on what constitutes the public interest.[7] It is a useful concept, to be sure. For you to say, "Air pollution control is in the public interest," is a short, convenient way to say that air pollution is bad not just for you but for many other people and that you think the gains from control of air pollution would be worth their cost. That kind of

[6] In the light of this discussion, Plato's proposal for policy making by a philosopher-king can be appreciated as being more than a quaint proposal for a benevolent dictator. Plato did not draw the contemporary distinction between fact and value. If he used modern terminology, he would presumably say that what we now call values are a sub-category of facts. By observing man's nature, Plato believed, one could discover man's purpose in the universe. Speaking very roughly, *purpose* serves the same role in Plato's thinking as end-of-the-line values serve in much contemporary thinking.

Because, then, everything that an analyst needs to know in order to reach a policy conclusion is knowable (since, to repeat, man's purpose is knowable), a sufficiently powerful and industrious analytic mind could conclusively choose policies. The correct policy is not a matter of dispute; there would be no need for political controversy about it. Hence the policy choices of that powerful analytic mind could happily serve Plato's hypothetical ideal republic.

Would it matter which philosopher is king? Any mind powerful enough to work through the analysis of ideal social policy would be satisfactory. And no one without a sufficiently powerful mind would be recognizable as a philosopher. Since all sufficiently powerful minds would come to the same policy conclusions (for correct policy is a matter of fact), it makes no difference which philosopher is king.

[7] A useful exposition of the various meanings of the "public interest" is W. A. R. Leys and C. M. Perry, *Philosophy and the Public Interest* (Chicago: Committee To Advance Original Work in Philosophy, 1959).

17

statement, however, does not mean that anyone agrees with you on the value of air pollution control. "Public interest" does not denote an agreed-upon interest; it only denotes what is, in someone's opinion, good for the public.

Sometimes "public interest" is used to refer to the common good—that is, to values that could be agreed to by almost everyone in the society and that would therefore not be disputed by informed and rational men. One view in political philosophy is that, since the universe is a cosmos (that is, orderly and harmonious), the common good encompasses all legitimate values that we might pursue in political life.[8] A more common contemporary view is that since the universe is *not* harmonious, values that can be agreed to are only some fraction of all the values we might pursue; on other values men will inevitably be in conflict. Either way, however, we do not in fact know or agree on which values are embraced in the common good.

Whichever way we turn, these problems of clarifying and organizing values or goals remain intractable. On this count alone, the analysis of policy cannot conclusively settle a policy issue; and what the President wants, the Senate will oppose—or what you want I will oppose—because the disputing parties agree neither on values nor on precisely how they are to enter into their own respective analyses of policy.[9]

Resistance to Analysis

The limits on analysis that we have so far discussed are of a particular kind. They indicate how far man might go, *if he tried,* toward settling policy

[8] It runs through classical Greek philosophy. See the chapter on Plato and Aristotle in L. Strauss and J. Cropsey (eds.), *History of Political Philosophy* (Chicago: Rand McNally & Co., 1963).

[9] *Utility theory:* Sophisticated intellectual effort has gone into the search for agreed criteria for policy, a search that nevertheless continues to fail. A major line of inquiry has been utility theory. The eighteenth-century utilitarian Jeremy Bentham thought he had found in the principle "the greatest good for the greatest number" a criterion for policy analysis on which agreement should be possible. The egalitarian spirit of his principle was not universally acceptable. In addition, his principle was logically defective. For the greatest good cannot simultaneously be given to the greatest number; to give more privileges or benefits to A so that he can enjoy the greatest good is to withhold them from B.

Responding to the technical difficulty in the principle, economists explored the possibility that the maximization of total utility (of satisfaction) in society might be a universally acceptable criteria for policy. The best policy, they proposed, would be that which created the largest sum of want satisfaction in the society. They discovered their principle to be defective on many counts. Some people simply do not agree that want satisfaction is acceptable as a criteria; some wants, they think, ought not to be satisfied. And many people believe that some people's wants are less important than others', hence do not believe in simply maximizing want satisfaction, but instead wish to achieve some specific distribution of want satisfaction—a distribution in favor of, for example, Aryans, whites, Hindus, Europeans, the rich, the old families, proletarians, the landed aristocracy, and so forth.

Granted then that the maximization of utility (of want satisfaction) is an unacceptable criterion and granted that the distribution of utility in a population has to be specified in any utility criterion for policy, does there remain any significant possibility of finding some agreement on utility distribution that would extend the possibilities of analytic policy making? Present attempts to find an area of agreement—taking the form, at the hands of mathematical social scientists, of exploring conditions to be imposed upon the construction of a social-welfare function—continue to be unsuccessful. See K. J. Arrow, *Social Choice and Individual Values,* 2nd ed. (New York: John Wiley and Sons, Inc., 1963).

18

disputes by investigating their merits—that is, by studying and reasoning about policy instead of fighting over it. Often, however, he does not even try. Why?

Irrationality. Men turn an indifferent or hostile eye on policy analysis because they are not wholly rational. Because, specifically, it is easier to feel than to think. Because they cling to beliefs that serve the needs of their personalities. Because words or symbols with which they talk about politics come to be more dear to them than the things to which the symbols refer.[10] Because sometimes it pains them to change their minds. Because they have picked up all kinds of beliefs from their families, friends, churches, and other groups—beliefs that give them a comforting orientation to the world about them and which they consequently dare not challenge. Because it may not have occurred to them that policy analysis is of potential great value.

Our preoccupation in these chapters with exploring the possibilities of analysis should not blind us to man's mountainous indifference (and sometimes his troubled hostility) to it. Policy analysis of the kind we have been discussing seems destined never to go very far because men do not want it to.

Assaults on the mind. Moreover, man is forever assaulted by a barrage of communications from other men who want to manipulate him. If he wants to pursue analysis, or encourage those who do, he must fight off the seductive irrational and nonrational appeals of political parties, candidates for office, interest groups, and propagandists of other kinds. They everywhere tug at his attention and try to commit his mind before he has had time to think. They are always at his ear.

Men who "know" what they want. And those at his ear may not want to analyze policy either, for they may have decided that they already know what they want. Senator Joseph McCarthy wanted no analysis of the threat of internal communism in the U. S.; he wanted to proceed directly against a whole class of people he indiscriminately associated with communism, socialism, liberalism, and internationalism. Similarly, most taxpayers' councils scattered around the United States want only limited analysis of government fiscal policy; on their basic antagonism to government expenditures they have already made up their minds: on that issue, they feel, the less discussion and the less study, the better.

Reasoned grounds for rejection. Even those people most interested in analysis will know that analysis will always be influenced by the biases of the analysts and by their incompetences, and that hence it is not always to be trusted. And they will know that, since most analysis takes place in organizations, it will always be marred by organizational biases, rigidities, and other incompetence. Take for example the unhappy failure of organizations to define relevant problems. An organization like the Air Force is primarily established to exploit the usefulness of aircraft for national defense. Its policy problems therefore revolve around the question: How best to use aircraft for defense? As an organization, however, it is most unlikely ever to ask the question (which as time passes and new techniques of warfare are developed comes to be a critical question): Should aircraft give way to missiles? And the organization may even try to suppress the question elsewhere in the Department of Defense.

[10] See M. Edelman, *The Symbolic Uses of Politics* (Urbana, Ill.: University of Illinois Press, 1964).

Organizational obstacles to satisfactory analysis constitute a subject in themselves. Differences of rank in organizations obstruct communication; the generalist's rivalry with the specialist sows distrust and becomes a source of bias; the organization's hiring policies may not attract competent personnel; promotion may be based on fitting in with the organization rather than on analytical skill; and so on. No few examples, however, can represent the luxuriant variety of organizational barriers to analysis.[11]

WHO CAN BE TRUSTED?

Imagine that you have in your hands a lengthy policy analysis leading up to a specific policy proposal. Imagine also that, although you do not know it, it happens to be an analysis for which information is wholly adequate, that is not overly complex, that is not cut short because of time limits or because of the costliness of the analysis itself, and that is not to be disqualified because of any disagreement with the definition of the policy problem—in other words, that overcomes all the difficulties in evaluation that we have discussed. Would you endorse the policy recommended?

Not until you could confirm that it is in fact a complete and unflawed analysis—if even then. But how would you determine whether it is? You will have neither time nor competence to study the analysis. Should you trust the analyst blindly? Obviously not. Ask someone who is competent to give you an opinion as to whether the analysis is complete and unflawed? But how to find a competent person, and how to know whether he is competent? Ask someone competent to judge him? But then how . . . ?

Thus, even those who would like to see more analysis in policy making will not wholly endorse it, will never wholly accept its results, and will obviously want some kind of political machinery to make policy decisions, with all that implies for "politics" in policy making.

[11] For a survey and analysis, see H. L. Wilensky, *Organizational Intelligence* (New York: Basic Books, 1967), pp. 175–178.

Limits on Policy Analysis

Making
the Most
of Analysis

If beyond some limits the policy analyst inevitably founders
in a bog of complexity, and cannot find satisfactory
criteria for a reasoned solution, nevertheless he has ingeniously
picked up many techniques to stretch his capacities.
They are all the more important because a group of them
change in surprising ways the character of policy analysis.

Many of man's elementary cultural accomplishments are, of course, methods of extending his problem-solving capacities. Think of archetypal man. Beyond speech itself, what has he devised, discovered, or blundered onto that has significantly enlarged his problem-solving capacity, and hence his capacity to analyze public policy? One might first mention a written language, with all that it implies for the possibility of communication, for storage of information, and for so precious a gain as recording solutions so that man can be spared the trouble of having to solve the same problems over and over again. Secondly, one might think of quantification, for without the skill in measurement and comparison that numbers make possible, man's mind would be crippled. Thirdly, one might mention "factoring out"—that is, dividing a problem into parts that can be independently analyzed.[1]

Other powerful extenders of man's analytical capacities are specific processes for formal rigorous analysis: mathematics and logic, and the whole collection of sophisticated techniques subsumed under the term "scientific method." One can add to this list by further detailing. For example: probability theory, through which man has extraordinarily extended his capacity to cope with inadequate information and an uncertain future; the powerful tool of double-entry bookkeeping, developed in about the thirteenth century; high-speed electronic computation, an accomplishment of the twentieth century; and the techniques mentioned in Chapter Two.

Clearly, the limits on analytic policy making are in some large part culturally determined. And the limits are probably receding somewhat faster than ever before. The use of complex written languages and of special codes for information storage, for example, is still only in its infancy. At the hands of mathematicians, formal analytical techniques are growing apace. Moreover, we are increasingly coming to perceive that "the scientific method" is less a name for a standardized set of investigatory techniques than for an expanding universe of them.[2]

It is hard to know where to stop looking for devices that stretch man's analytic capacities. For example, a serious emergency, a crisis, often has the effect of transforming a policy analyst's perceptions (and sometimes also of galvanizing his energies), with the result that he gets a new grasp on his problem.[3] If usually we think of a crisis as something to be avoided, some kinds of crises can be produced deliberately in order to stimulate the policy maker. Annual budgeting, for example, can be managed to create an annual

---

[1] An unusually perceptive and stimulating analysis of precisely how "factoring out" or subdividing problems aids rationality is in H. A. Simon, "The Architecture of Complexity," 106 *Proceedings of the American Philosophical Society* (December, 1962).

[2] C. W. Churchman, *Prediction and Optimal Decision* (Englewood Cliffs, N. J.: Prentice-Hall, Inc., 1961). See also R. E. Lane, "The Decline of Politics and Ideology In A Knowledgeable Society," 31 *American Sociological Review* (October, 1966).

[3] For strengths and weaknesses of crisis decision-making, see H. C. Hart, "Crisis, Community, and Consent in Water Politics," 22 *Law and Contemporary Problems* (Winter, 1957). See also, on the possibility that crisis improves the decision capacity of organizations, H. L. Wilensky, *Organizational Intelligence* (New York: Basic Books, Inc., 1967), pp. 76f.

Making the Most of Analysis

crisis; it can compel a policy maker to reach major decisions under a sometimes frightening time pressure.

Ideology

Ideology is a conspicuous specialized aid to the analysis of public policy. A troublesome word, "ideology" has come to mean many things. It may denote any interlocked set of important generalizations about social organization, like the American ideology that associates ideas about democracy, liberty, pluralism, private enterprise, individualism, and social responsibility in a way that guides an American's thinking about public policy. Or it may denote a more formal and highly organized set of such beliefs, like the Marxist-Leninist principles that give a good deal of guidance to policy in the U.S.S.R. and Communist China. Some people who use the term would say, however, that Marxism-Leninism is an ideology not because it is formal and highly organized but because, in addition, it constitutes a set of principles guiding the transformation of society. In their view, "ideology" always refers to a set of revolutionary ideas.[4]

All that we mean to say here is that any even loosely organized set of interlocking generalizations or principles about social organization—or, more specifically, about politico-economic organization—is of enormous help to policy analysis; and probably it is indispensable.[5] It appears that all policy analysis rests to a degree on ideology so defined. A working commitment, even if not dogmatic, to pluralist democracy and corporate enterprise, for example, permits a policy analyst greatly to restrict his search for policies and generally to simplify his analysis so that he can better grasp it.

In effect an ideology takes certain beliefs out of the gunfire of criticism— or at least throws up some argument to defend them. These beliefs, verification of which would require impossible feats of fact-gathering and analysis, can therefore be introduced into policy analysis as though they were settled fact.

What if the beliefs are mistaken? Even mistaken beliefs can serve to organize and simplify policy analysis. Whether the American faith in private enterprise is mistaken or not, we tend to analyze monopoly policy on the assumption of private enterprise, and we reach conclusions that are helpful to the determination of policy. The policies may be mistaken; but if, because we share a common set of assumptions, we believe them to be correct, we accept them. All that we in effect ask of analysis is that it take us from the assumption, which is to be left unquestioned, to a policy.

If the ideology is far enough from fact, however, it can cripple policy analysis. It may generate agreed-on policies that nevertheless do not work—as, for example, our budget-balancing policies at the onset of the Great Depression of the thirties. Ideologically correct, they prolonged the Depression rather than shortened it.

The explicitness, detail, and completeness of communist ideology in

[4] For comparison of American and Soviet ideologies, see Z. Brzezinski and S. P. Huntington, *Political Power: USA/USSR* (New York: Viking Press, Inc., 1963), pp. 17–24, 35–70.

[5] A now classic analysis of the usefulness of ideology is K. Mannheim, *Ideology and Utopia* (New York: Harcourt, Brace and World, Inc., 1936).

China or the Soviet Union simplify analysis much more than do the looser ideologies of democratic systems. When the incompleteness of a democratic ideology compels the policy analyst to investigate practical virtues and defects of competing policy alternatives, a communist policy maker will sometimes find that his ideology gives him a reasonably full justification for a policy choice. Policy analysis may therefore be quicker and surer in a communist society, but the risks of policy error derived directly from mistaken ideology are correspondingly greater.

Strategies or Dodges

It is not, however, man's use of language, of quantification, of other universal tools, or of ideology that changes the character of policy analysis in surprising ways. We begin to see a somewhat unexpected new face on policy analysis only when we look at certain strategies or dodges that man has developed for dealing with very complex problems—strategies that are especially well adapted to public policy analysis. Some of the most important are as follows:

SATISFICING

In the conventional ideal of a rational decision, a decision maker maximizes something—utility or want satisfaction, income, national security, the general welfare, or some other such value. But, as we have already noted, an exhaustive search for the maximum, for the best of all possible policies, is not usually worth what it costs, and may in fact be impossible of accomplishment. An alternative strategy, therefore, is not to try too hard—to decide instead on some acceptable level of goal accomplishment short of maximization, and then pursue the search until a policy is found that attains that level. One "satisfices" instead of maximizes.[6]

THE NEXT CHANCE

Sometimes policy analysts deliberately make little mistakes to avoid big ones. One can deliberately choose a policy (knowing that it is not quite the right policy) that leaves open the possibility of doing better in a next step, instead of a policy designed to be on target but difficult to amend. While an Indian civil servant, for example, is inclined to shoot for his target with little thought of a second chance, an American civil servant never expects to be wholly right and values a second chance. In as relatively simple a policy problem as routing New Haven traffic, to try out one-way traffic going south and stand ready, if that is unsuccessful, to try a northbound flow may be better than to gamble, through an *a priori* study of traffic flows, on a permanent installation of expensive controls to inaugurate southbound one-way movement.

FEEDBACK

A policy analyst may want to deal inconclusively with a problem—that is, keep a next chance open because he thinks that with the passage of time he will come to know more. But if he can choose a policy that will, as in the traffic example, itself feed back information necessary to a better choice of

[6] The word and the concept are from H. A. Simon, "A Behavioral Model of Rational Choice," 69 *Quarterly Journal of Economics* (February, 1955).

Making the Most of Analysis

policy, so much the better. Policy feedback is of course a commonplace phenomenon: it is hard to imagine a policy that feeds back no useful information at all. Monetary and fiscal policy is an example of especially quick and powerful feedback because of its immediate impact on business activity. But policy-making systems differ in sensitivity to feedback and in the skill with which they choose policies in order to induce feedback. A policy chosen because it is ideologically correct—like Soviet policy on collective farms—may persist for years in spite of failure, with its advocates blind to feedback.[7]

REMEDIALITY

In the classical model of rational decision making a policy analyst concerned about American Negroes would be required to formulate in his mind an organized set of policy aspirations and to specify for various dates in the future the income, educational, status, and other social and cultural goals at which policy should aim. In actual fact, some policy analysts greatly simplify this otherwise impossible goal-setting task by refusing to look very far ahead—focusing instead on the removal of all-too-observable disadvantages now suffered by the Negroes. That is, if they cannot decide with any precision the state of affairs they want to achieve, they can at least specify the state of affairs from which they want to escape. They deal more confidently with what is wrong than with what in the future may or may not be right.

Critics will say that policy would be more rational if it were guided by positive instead of negative objectives, but it is not at all certain that positive objectives could win assent, or that they would be as operational as negative objectives. It is not clear what sort of policies should now be chosen to achieve such an objective as equality for the Negro, but what is required to ameliorate his generally poor housing, schooling, and job-opportunity situations, as well as his being on the short end of some of the most egregious forms of social discrimination *is* reasonably clear—even if we do not know or agree on what ideal housing, education, job markets, and social relations are. Similarly, in another context, the government of India does not know much about how to get high production from its farmers, but it does know how to go about eliminating some of the obvious obstacles to production, such as poor seeds, inadequate water supplies, and a price structure that discourages initiative. If in this sense policy analysts look backward instead of forward, they sometimes gain rather than lose competence.

SERIALITY

A policy analyst who appreciates a next chance, exploits feedback, and keeps his eye on ills to be remedied will come to take for granted that policy making is typically serial, or sequential. He will see that policy making is typically a never-ending process of successive steps in which continual nibbling is a substitute for a good bite. He will design policy not merely on the expectation of a second step but on the projection of a third, or a fourth—of an

[7] Feedback as an aid to decision making has been given its most precise formulation by those who have tried to describe social processes generally as communications processes, taking their lead from N. Wiener, *The Human Use of Human Beings* (Boston: Houghton Mifflin Company, 1950). For a brief formulation of theory of this type, see K. W. Deutsch, *The Nerves of Government* (New York: The Free Press, 1963), Ch. 5, "A Simple Cybernetic Model."

Making the Most of Analysis

endless series. In this style of policy analysis, he sees possibilities for revising both policies and objectives, and he comes to treat policy making as open-ended in all its aspects. He and any political system of this style may therefore develop a high level of flexibility, resilience, and pertinacity that greatly raises his or its ability to make good policy in the face of complexity. In a system in which policy making is frankly recognized to be serial or sequential, the whole system may be tailored to rapid sequences so that, though no one policy move is great, the frequency of small moves makes rapid social change possible.

In the U.S., policy analysts nibble endlessly at taxation, social security, national defense, conservation, foreign aid, and the like. Policy analysts assume that these problems are never solved, and hold themselves in readiness to return to them again and again. That kind of persistence in policy making has transformed the society. America, observers say, has gone through an industrial revolution, an organizational revolution, a revolution in economic organization (from *laissez faire* to a highly regulated economy), and a revolution in the role of the family—but all through policy sequences so undramatic as to obscure the magnitude of change.

BOTTLENECKS

Every policy analyst—and you and I in our personal problems—makes frequent use of the tactic of bottleneck breaking to simplify complex problems. On a superficial view of policy making, a bottleneck is nothing more than clear evidence of a breakdown in decision making. If something is running behind schedule, or something necessary to action is missing, or there is a congestion, we say a bottleneck exists. But since bottlenecks are inevitable for complex policy making, policy analysts have discovered how to use them to make the best of a less-than-ideal situation.

Wartime planning of the allocation of labor and other resources is a dramatic example. It was not possible in World War II for the American government to achieve a comprehensive control over resource allocation for staffing, supplying, and producing for the military services; the task was too complex. Allocations were therefore planned around the bottlenecks—the scarcest of the resources. The Controlled Materials Plan was organized around steel, copper, and aluminum. In addition, as other bottlenecks appeared, as they did in rubber and transportation, the President appointed temporary "czars" to do whatever necessary to adjust other resources demands and supplies to the bottleneck items. In the U. K., where labor was an especially scarce item, much of wartime resource planning was in labor allocations.[8]
allocations.[8]

At an extreme, one can see the two contrasting possibilities for policy analysis: on the one hand, plan everything to fit with everything else; on the other, plan to break specific bottlenecks as they arise. The first is impossible; the second, though far from ideal, works.

INCREMENTALISM

Usually—though not always—what is feasible politically is policy only incrementally, or marginally, different from existing policies. Drastically different

[8] D. Novick, M. Anshen, and W. C. Truppner, *Wartime Production Controls* (New York: Columbia University Press, 1949), Ch. 8; and Ely Devons, *Planning in Practice* (Cambridge, England: The University Press, 1950).

Making the Most of Analysis

policies fall beyond the pale. That aside, a preoccupation with no more than incremental or marginal changes in policy often serves for still other reasons to raise the level of competence of policy. Where applicable, such a strategy:

1. concentrates the policy-maker's analysis on familiar, better-known experience;
2. sharply reduces the number of different alternative policies to be explored, and
3. sharply reduces the number and complexity of factors he has to analyze.

For a regulation of industrial monopoly, for example, a policy analyst may be able to make analytic headway if he restricts his analysis, as does the Antitrust Division of the Department of Justice, to policies like present ones—to proposals, say, for new curbs on corporate mergers, or new restrictions on corporate price policies. For he will thus concentrate his attention on a not impossibly long list of policies. He will also be able to draw on a great deal of experience that the Antitrust Division and the courts have had with past controls over mergers and prices. And he will avoid the complex analysis of more sweeping changes like public ownership of corporate enterprise. On such a big policy change as public ownership, American experience has very little to offer him as a guide to his analysis.[9]

Significance of the Strategies

What is the ordinary interpretation put on these strategies or dodges? On superficial examination they are often dismissed as irrational. For they are seen as indecisiveness, patching up, timidity, triviality, narrowness of view, inconclusiveness, caution, and procrastination. But we have seen them to be useful devices for stretching man's analytic capacities. Man has had to be devilishly inventive to cope with the staggering difficulties he faces. His analytical methods cannot be restricted to tidy scholarly procedures. The piecemealing, remedial incrementalist or satisficer may not look like an heroic figure. He is nevertheless a shrewd, resourceful problem-solver who is wrestling bravely with a universe that he is wise enough to know is too big for him.

[9] All these strategies for extending the possibility of policy analysis are discussed at length in D. Braybrooke and C. E. Lindblom, *A Strategy of Decision* (New York: The Free Press, 1963). For an example of their application to a specific policy area, see A. Wildavsky, *The Politics of the Budgetary Process* (Boston: Little, Brown & Co., 1964). For a discussion of their usefulness in a variety of arenas of decision making, see A. Hirschman and C. E. Lindblom, "Economic Development, Research and Development, Policy Making: Some Converging Views," 7 *Behavioral Science* (April, 1962). For controversy about these strategies, see "Governmental Decision Making," a symposium, 24 *Public Administration Review* (September, 1964), pp. 153–165.

Making the Most of Analysis

PART TWO

The Play of Power

The Play
in Main
Outline

CHAPTER FIVE

We now come back to face up to the fact that, however extended, policy analysis is inadequate. If it is not possible through analysis to find policies that are everywhere accepted because proven to be correct, what can be done? Someone has to take on the task of deciding on policy for society. But because no one can perform the task of making a decision on policy without the "power" to do so, the more usual way to put the point is to say that, in the absence of universal agreement on what is to be done, someone has to either seize or be given "power" to decide.[1]

In actual fact, of course, "power" is always held by a number of persons rather than by one; *hence policy is made through the complex processes by which these persons exert power or influence over each other.* What is the character of this play of power in policy making? And how is policy analysis incorporated into it?

Observed Events and Underlying Process

The most obvious thing about the play of power is that it is exciting to play, and—when we can get a glimpse into its subtleties—fascinating to watch. We read of episodes like the following:[2]

. . . in the midst of the presidential campaign of 1948 President Truman asked Arthur Vandenberg, Republican leader on foreign policy, to "slip in the back door" of the White House for a "private chat" in the course of which the President expressed his appreciation of the "judicial" tone of a campaign speech by Vandenberg and observed that the retention of the bipartisan foreign policy was more important than "who was elected President."

. . . in the 1953 battle by the Eisenhower Administration to obtain a brief extension of the excess profits tax, Representative Daniel A. Reed, chairman of the Ways and Means Committee, . . . declined to bring the bill to a vote in his committee. To pry the bill from his committee, the Republican leadership pushed through the Rules Committee a resolution to call up the measure despite the lack of committee action. With this threat over his head, Reed called a meeting of his committee which voted down his ruling that consideration of the bill was not in order and reported the bill for passage.

President Kennedy to persons urging policies on him: "I agree but I don't know whether the government will agree."

Why the coy and obviously only figurative reference to Vandenberg's entering by the back door? Are we to understand that the President was going to propose a conspiracy to the Senator? Or merely that he hoped to establish a relationship of personal confidence? If the latter, why? In what one might think is a tough play of power, is there much use for velvet gloves? Why is a bipartisan foreign policy more important than a bipartisan domestic policy, which the President did not urge on Senator Vandenberg?

If President Eisenhower wanted to extend the excess profits tax, why would Reed, a Republican leader in the House, so stubbornly refuse? Why no coordination? Why would Reed go so far as to force other party leaders to gang up on him? How did they manage it? If Reed's committee was willing to go along with the President, why was not Reed earlier compelled by his own

[1] The term "power" has been placed within quotation marks to express some uncertainty as to what the word means. It will remain undefined, but its meaning will become increasingly clear as we use it. For analysis of the concept, see R. A. Dahl, *Modern Political Analysis,* Foundations of Modern Political Science Series (Englewood Cliffs, N.J.: Prentice-Hall, Inc., 1963), Ch. 5.

[2] V. O. Key, Jr., *Politics, Parties, and Pressure Groups* (New York: Thomas Y. Crowell Company, 1960), pp. 248n, 721n; President Kennedy is quoted in J. K. Galbraith, *The New Industrial State* (Boston: Houghton Mifflin Company, 1967).

committee to go along. What powers did he have over them, and they over him?

What did President Kennedy mean by "the government"? Is it, whatever it is, beyond the President's control, as he implied? What kinds of powers (and whose), if any, are beyond Presidential control?

Useful as these glimpses into recent history are, they raise more questions than they answer. What is described as happening in each case can be understood in the light of certain underlying mechanisms or processes in the play of power in policy making. It is these that we want to lay bare. We can begin with the main outline of them. In practically all countries:

I. The play of power is a process of cooperation among specialists.

II. The play of power is not a substitute for policy analysis, simply resolving those issues left unsettled by analysis. Instead, policy analysis is incorporated as an instrument or weapon into the play of power, changing the character of analysis as a result.

III. The play of power proceeds, for the most part, according to rule; it is gamelike.

We shall develop these three propositions in a preliminary way in this chapter, with substantial documentation, as well as further specification, in subsequent chapters. They are central to the entire analysis.

Cooperation Among Specialists

SPECIALIZATION

As we have just said, in no political system are the tasks of policy making given over to or seized by any one person; in all political systems they are given over to or seized by many persons. The tasks come to be specialized. Except in small political systems that can be run by something like a New England town meeting, not all citizens can be the immediate, or *proximate*, makers of policy. They yield the immediate (or proximate) task of decision to a small minority.[3]

The proximate policy makers are of course themselves specialized: members of the House of Representatives, Senators, President, appointed administrative officials of various kinds, and some party leaders. Each performs a policy-making task different from that of any other.

Classifying in a different way, there are specialized tasks to be per-

[3] Giving the word "proximate" a somewhat unusual meaning, we shall define *proximate policy makers* as those participants who are "closest" or most proximate to the actual making of a decision. They are those who share immediate legal authority to decide on specific policies, together with other immediate participants in policy decisions, like top party leaders, to whom the above have conceded extra-legal authority or who, for any other reason, are strong and immediate participators in actual decisions on policy— excluding, however, any of the above legal authorities who waive their control over decisions in favor of others (for example, a figurehead mayor who does what the party boss tells him).

Leaders are the above, together with other persons who, though not proximate policy makers, exert significantly more influence on the proximate policy makers than do ordinary citizens and voters (for example, an interest-group leader, an influential editor or writer, or a party leader who does not enter the circle of proximate policy makers).

The Play in Main Outline

formed: initiating, vetoing, coordinating, planning, establishing general constraints on the alternatives to be considered, widening the range of choice, stimulating new policy ambitions, adjudicating conflicting intentions, and controlling through the purse-strings. An interest-group leader, for example, can initiate consideration of a policy but he cannot carry a decision through without the concurrence of a government official. The "man with an idea" outside of government, not among the proximate policy makers, may control their views. Marx is the most dramatic case.[4]

COOPERATION

If only I can initiate and only you can veto, who makes policy? If your ideas form my mind but I hold office and you do not, who makes policy? It makes more sense to ask "What makes policy?" For if there are many specialists, each performing his differentiated task in policy making, policy can be made only through cooperation among them. In a democratic polity, voters exercise their powers to choose proximate policy makers, whom they then count on to do *their* jobs. An interest-group leader enters into an interchange with voters; he needs their attention and they need his information. Party leaders use their power to reduce a multiplicity of issues to a few so that the choice before voters is not impossibly complex; they are aware that voters need this help if voters are to do their part. Prime minister, president, governor, and mayor cannot perform their tasks without the cooperation, respectively, of parliament, congress, assembly, and councilmen. And vice-versa.

We are not so naïve as to ask, "Who makes automobiles in the U.S.?" unless we intend to be satisfied with the name of a process or institution; we do not expect one or a few persons to be named. We know that thousands of people are directly engaged, and millions indirectly, in making cars. Even if we group these thousands or millions together by categories, we do not look for a simple-minded answer. We know that workers make cars. But managers do, too. And so do machines, and builders of the machines, and suppliers of parts, and workers who make the parts. About automobiles, we are sophisticated enough to know that to answer the question, "Who makes them?" we would have to explain *the complex ways in which all these cooperate with each other*. We need a similar sophistication to understand the making of policy.

COOPERATION AND CONFLICT

A cynic might believe that to say that policy makers need to cooperate is simply a euphemistic way of saying that they must reconcile conflict. Not at all. Admittedly, the notion that politics *is* conflict resolution is deeply embedded in political science.[5] One can indeed imagine government's serving the dominant purpose of preventing man's violence to his fellow man and his appropriation of his neighbor's property or wife, believing that in the absence

[4] Keynes' impact on economic policy is another example. New testimony to his impact is in *New Dimensions of Political Economy* (Cambridge: Harvard University Press, 1966), by Walter Heller, former Chairman of the President's Council of Economic Advisers.

[5] For example, H. Lasswell, *Politics: Who Gets What, When, How?* (Cleveland: World Publishing Co., 1958); and conflict resolution in the form of "value allocation" in D. Easton, *A Framework For Political Analysis* (Englewood Cliffs, N. J.: Prentice-Hall, Inc., 1965).

The Play in Main Outline

of government men would struggle with each other in the "war of all against all" envisaged by Thomas Hobbes.[6] The fact is, however, that governments do a great deal more than adjudicate the kind of conflict that would make life intolerable in the absence of government. For once governments are established, it is apparent to everyone that they are instruments for vast tasks of social cooperation. Governments are used to build roads, dam rivers, irrigate the land, encourage manufacturing, facilitate commerce through creating and regulating a money supply, care for the aged and disabled, explore new lands, and educate the children.

These tasks require complex positive feats of cooperation, not only in implementation but in the policy-making processes through which they are decided on. Whether children are to be educated by public authority is itself a big question. How they are to be educated raises many more questions. Not surprisingly, big questions like these are not turned over to any one policy maker but require cooperation in policy making among many persons, including the ordinary citizen himself in democratic states.

To be sure, one can describe the task of ensuring cooperation among policy makers in the language of conflict resolution, saying that policy makers must resolve their conflicts in order to agree on policy. Indeed they must. The important thing to be understood, however, is that conflicts are largely those that spring from the opportunities for cooperation that abound once political life becomes orderly. Men are thrown into conflict largely because they have seized or have had assigned to them specialized roles in a complex cooperative process in which many others must play complementary roles.

Policy Analysis Subordinated to the Play of Power

How do policy makers cooperate? One method, it turns out, is through policy analysis—employed, however, to make analysis an instrument of the play of power, not an alternative to it. This fact adds a new dimension to the analysis discussed in the preceding chapters. Here it would be handy if we could say everything at once, but we shall have to sort out the intricacies, point by point, of analysis as it enters into the play of power.

To begin: an obvious answer to the question, "How do policy makers cooperate?", is that they persuade each other to agree. Persuasion can take a rich variety of forms: outright deceit and irrational and non-rational appeals of many kinds, including, at one extreme, organized propaganda, and at the other, exploited ties of kinship and friendship.[7]

In the relatively direct relations of proximate policy makers to each other, these techniques of persuasion are by themselves inadequate. They are employed, but they are not enough. Even ordinary citizens will to a degree (some to a very slight degree) see through these techniques of persuasion and will therefore refuse to be moved until something more convincing is brought to bear on them.

[6] In *Leviathan,* Ch. 13.

[7] Political persuasion is a profession and an industry—in the form of public relations. For example, Whitaker and Baxter and associated firms were paid three-quarters of a million dollars by the American Medical Association for their professional services in a three-and-a-half-year campaign against health insurance begun in 1948; and all together the AMA poured almost $5 million into the campaign (S. Kelley, Jr., *Professional Public Relations and Propaganda* [Baltimore: Johns Hopkins Press, 1956], p. 106).

The Play in Main Outline

A powerful additional technique of persuasion—its ubiquity to be documented in later chapters—is policy analysis by one policy maker to find a way in which a policy he desires can serve the values of another policy maker to whom the persuasion is directed. The President fears that Congress will cut aid to Latin America. His most effective means of inducing Congress not to cut may be to find a value that he believes stirs congressmen—like restraining the spread of communism in Latin America—and show them how aid achieves that value. His own interest in aid may be quite different. There might not even be one common problem to which President and Congress think aid is a possible solution. It is enough that he can influence them by analysis designed to connect *his* desired policy with *their* fundamental dispositions or values.

Why is analysis of this kind so powerful a persuader? Why, when *A* tries to persuade *B*, does *B* listen so respectfully? It follows from what has been said in earlier chapters about the complexity of policy issues that no policy maker can be secure in his policy positions. *B* may be firmly anchored in a set of general attitudes or principles—to which he has turned either dogmatically or merely because he sees the need for some firm general guidance to his thinking. But he will have to realize that what policy best serves his purposes is always a matter of dispute and that what is good policy today may not be good tomorrow.

If *B* favors a tax cut to increase consumer spending to head off a recession, he knows that, depending on circumstances and an uncertain future, increased public spending might turn out to be a better way of stimulating spending. And if he favors either policy for increasing spending today, he knows that, almost overnight, inflationary tendencies may require an about-face in policy—a dampening down of spending rather than a stimulation. Summer of 1967 was marked by just these uncertainties about economic policy, and no policy maker could claim he could be sure about what was required. Under these circumstances every *B* is vulnerable to new information and analysis from every *A*. *B* will be open to, if not grasping for, new facts and new insights on policy choices before him.

Officials and other leaders whose reputations can be won or lost by the success or failures of policies they choose can hardly afford not to listen. Moreover, if their opponents are armed with analysis, they must be so armed, too.

In the chapters to come, we will see specific evidence of dependence on partisan analysis. For a preliminary overview of this kind of analysis, however, further key features are:

1. For the policy maker who practices it, it serves to clarify his own policy preferences. For the very reasons that *B* is receptive to analysis, so also is *A*. If an interest-group leader, legislator, or party leader searches for features of his desired policy that suit the general value position of others whom he wishes to persuade, it will occur to him that his policy may not be the only one that could attain his own values or goals. Perhaps he can find another that will suit both him and those he wishes to persuade. Hence his use of this kind of analysis both pulls others toward him and pushes him toward others.

2. This kind of analysis is not frustrated, as in much of the analysis discussed

33

The Play in Main Outline

in earlier chapters, by lack of agreement on policy goals, for it does not challenge the values of the policy maker to whom it is addressed. The President, we saw, does not need to ask whether he agrees with Congressional values on Latin-American aid; all he has to do is to find Congressional values in the light of which he can show that his policy is what Congress really wants.

3. But partisan analysis is not simply a method of rationalizing, of proving the merits of what has already been decided on? For, in the first place, it is not an effective tool of persuasion unless it discovers a connection between a given set of goals or attitudes and a policy to serve them. And, secondly, because it is practiced on others and self simultaneously, it serves as much to find a new position as to prove the merits of one already taken.

4. It does not need to be conclusive, in the sense of demonstrating that a policy in question is the correct or best policy; it need only go so far as to persuade a voter, legislator, prime minister, or administrator with respect to what he should do about the decision task he faces. And insofar as it is designed by a policy maker to clarify his own position, it need only go so far as to persuade the policy maker himself.

5. Hence this kind of analysis is clearly a kind subordinated to the play of power, and not an alternative to it. It does not avoid fighting over policy; it is a method of fighting.

6. Finally, this kind of analysis makes use of all the devices for extending analytical capacity discussed in the preceding chapter. But it does not suffer from quite all the disabilities of analysis described in Chapter Three. In particular, as already noted, it can be practiced in the absence of agreement on values, as well as in the absence, for any one analyst, of a clearly formulated and wholly satisfactory set of values such as is aspired to in the kind of nonpartisan analysis discussed in the earlier chapters.

Rules to Assign Tasks and Regulate the Play

When persuasion fails, what then? How then to achieve cooperation? The answer is: Through the exercise of power in the narrower sense of the term. This is to say, not through the influence or "power" of persuasion, but by means of stronger forms of power—possibly of highly coercive power.

When policy making is seen as a play of power going well beyond mutual persuasion, it is also sometimes mistakenly seen as somehow escaping deliberate human design. Power, some people will say, rests in the hands of the strong, the rich, the predatory, the white, the vested interests, or the "60 families"; and—come what may—policy making will, they believe, reflect the basic social power of such groups.[8]

We shall in a later chapter discuss elitist theories of policy making. Here we want only to make the point that the play of power in policy making is not a slam-bang imposition of will on will; it is instead—even in totalitarian systems—a game-like process in which *power is exerted according to man-made rule*. Anticipating some conclusions to be reached later, we allege here that the power of various social groups like the rich or the whites is less a determinant of policy outcomes than itself a result of the rules that men have made to govern the policy-making process.

[8] For examples, F. Lundberg, *America's Sixty Families* (New York: The Vanguard Press, 1937); R. S. and H. M. Lynch, *Middletown* (New York: Harcourt, Brace and Co., 1929); J. Burnham, *The Managerial Revolution* (New York: The John Day Co., 1941); and C. W. Mills, *The Power Elite* (New York: Oxford University Press, 1956).

The Play in Main Outline

Imagine a man who, in a revolutionary breakdown of orderly government, claims supreme power over policy. Will anyone take him seriously? Not if he has to enforce every single request for cooperation or obedience with his own fists or gun. There are too many other fists and guns. To make his claim to power credible, he needs some helping fists and guns; but they are of no help to him if he must in each case use his own fists and gun to compel their cooperation. He therefore needs, as a minimum, fists and guns that will accept a *rule* of obedience to him; fists and guns that will take orders from him without his having in each case to compel it.

He will also need a staff to help him make policy. How can he induce their cooperation in working out policy solutions to the many problems to which he cannot give personal attention? He cannot take time to intervene in each case with his fists and gun. Again, he cannot survive unless he can find policy makers who will cooperate by rule. The rules both assign tasks and assign powers to perform the assigned tasks. Rules specify what each participant in policy making can and cannot do, as well as what he must do, whom he must obey, and whom (if anyone) he can command.

Brezhnev, Kosygin, and their close associates win the cooperation of other Russian government officials not because they flaunt a long and fearsome list of prospective penalties for disobedience every time they give an order (they do not) but because other officials have accepted a rule of obedience, as well as a set of rules specifying what they themselves must do. The President and Congress obey an order of the Supreme Court not because the Court has gunmen at its service but because they accept the rule that the Court can judge an act of President or Congress to be unconstitutional.

Webster says that a rule is "a prescribed guide for conduct, action . . .; a regulation."[9]

Some examples of rules are:

From the Bible and the common law: *Thou shalt not kill.*

From the U.S. Constitution: *The executive power shall be vested in a President of the United States of America.*

By customary moral obligation: *Between political leaders, a political favor should be repaid with a political favor.*

From the U. S. Courts: *Congress may regulate the political conduct of government employees.*

Rules are:

Both general and specific to politics. "Thou shalt not kill" is a rule of universal applicability that constrains policy makers along with everyone else.

[9] Of many kinds of rules governing behavior, we are concerned, of course, only with those that regulate the play of power in policy making. The rule, "U. S. citizens must pay income taxes," is not such a rule; it is instead no more than a rule that announces policy. But the rule, "Tax legislation originates in the House and must be voted by both Senate and House, as well as approved by the President," is such a rule, for it governs what policy makers can and cannot do.

The Play in Main Outline

But constitutional and judicial rules, for example, are specialized to politics, like the rule above that vests the executive functions of government in the President.

Both legal and extra-legal. Many of the rules that organize the policy-making process are legally enacted. The U. S. Constitution is a large collection of them, and thousands more are to be found in legislative acts, administrative rulings, executive orders, and judicial decisions. But we shall see many examples of informal rules surrounding each legal rule or independent of legal rule.

Sometimes displaced by habitual behavior. The play of power takes some of its characteristics from habitual modes of behavior, quite aside from rule-regulated behavior. People fall into certain regularities of behavior not because they feel obligated by internal or external rules but for other reasons. Perhaps most of us refrain from mutilating each other not so much because law or moral code forbids it but because the very thought is revolting.

WHY ARE RULES OBEYED?

It is a rule in the British House of Commons that policy proposals of the Prime Minister are to be accepted by members of his party (the majority party) so long as they acknowledge him as party leader. Why? Not because the Prime Minister hires bully boys to enforce it, nor because any member of Parliament can be fined or imprisoned if he violates it. In large part, the rule stands because the Members of Parliament find it convenient to do their policy-making business through such a rule. They voluntarily accept it. It is a rule in the House of Representatives that a bill will usually be brought to the floor of the House for action only by decision of the House Rules Committee. Why? Because House members think that some rule is necessary and that such a rule permits them to do their work better than if they followed another rule.

Even in a democracy, however, rule keeping is not wholly voluntary. Not every official defeated for re-election voluntarily accepts the rule that he must vacate. He nevertheless accepts the rule for fear of losing his reputation if he challenges it, for fear of desertion by his staff, or for fear that others who accept the rule can command the military or the police to pick him up in his chair and carry him out to a parking lot. He may not even pause to ask whether and how the rule can be enforced on him; he may simply assume that somehow it can and will be.

At an extreme, a policy maker may accept a rule—say, a rule that he must obey the directives of the Communist Party—out of fear of imprisonment, torture, exile, or death. But the more common case in any system, aside from voluntarism, is obedience simply because disobedience would incapacitate a policy maker in his relations with other policy makers who play the game by rule.

Take note, too, that when one or a few policy makers propose to break the rules, the others can easily curb them by proceeding against them according to rules prescribing what shall be done in the case of rule violation. If the President should call on the Army to adjourn Congress indefinitely so that he could rule alone, it is unlikely that the Army would obey; and in any case it is almost certain that rules governing impeachment and removal of the President from office would be called into play by appropriate officials. In

The Play in Main Outline

short, policy-making is by rule, and so also is rule enforcement, where explicit enforcement is necessary.[10]

As a consequence, the play of power in policy making is not as rough, harsh, violent and bloody, even in authoritarian states, as might be supposed. It becomes so only if and when the whole web of rules begins to tear, as in 1967 in Communist China, or in the transformation to a new set of rules, as in the Bolshevik Revolution of 1917.

The Rule Called "Authority"

An especially important rule, it may have already been noticed, is the kind that does not directly lay down what a person can or cannot do except to say that he must do whatever some specified other person tells him to do. Some of our examples have been of that kind of rule. Such a rule establishes authority. To put the point in the form of a definition:

X has authority over Y *if* Y follows the rule that he obey X.[11]

If X controls Y by offering in each specific decision some reward to him, threatening him, or physically constraining him, he does not have authority over him. If Y obeys only when he sees merit in the specific command given him, X does not have authority over him. But if X can routinely exert power or influence over Y because Y accepts a rule that he obey, then X has authority over Y.

Authority is specific. Even so powerful a proximate policy maker as the President of the United States has, however, only limited authority. For example, he cannot adjourn Congress or remove Supreme Court justices.

Authority is a concession from those who are asked to obey. The rule that establishes authority is a rule of behavior for the person who is controlled, not a rule of behavior for the controller. You have no authority over me until I decide to follow, for whatever reason, the rule of obedience to you.

It is conceded for a variety of reasons. Since "authority" refers to a rule, what we have said above about why rules are accepted and obeyed also explains why people grant authority. As with other rules, authority is often voluntarily conceded.

[10] And so also, as we have seen, the specification and assignment of specialized policy-making tasks is achieved by rules.

[11] For a fuller exposition of authority as we have defined it, see H. A. Simon, D. W. Smithburg, and V. A. Thompson, *Public Administration* (New York: Alfred A. Knopf, 1959), Ch. 8. Some social scientists define authority differently. For example, Dahl, *Modern Political Analysis,* pp. 28–32. They say: X has authority over Y if Y acknowledges the legitimacy of X's controlling him. Or X has authority over Y if Y acknowledges an obligation to obey him. There is no point in quarreling over the difference in definition. That Y's accepting such a rule logically implies that he concedes legitimacy to X's control is an allegation on which we need not take a position. Many German citizens who abhorred Nazism accepted a rule of obedience to the Nazi government. It seems unnecessary for our purposes to ask whether in some sense or other that means that they did or did not concede legitimacy to their rulers. We will say that they conceded authority to their rulers if they accepted a rule of obedience, as most of them did.

Indirect Uses of Authority

In 1954, President Eisenhower's Secretary of the Interior authorized the commencement of the Upper Colorado River Reclamation Project. Only thereafter the President was able to obtain Senate approval of the St. Lawrence Waterway project. Of the 10 senators from the area affected by the Colorado project, only two voted against the Waterway. Obviously the President succeeded in bringing the western senators around to his desired policy, but he did not do so through any authority over how senators should vote. What then was the source of his influence over them? It was his authority to begin the Colorado project (which had already earlier been authorized by Congress). He used his authority over that project to do a favor to western senators, who thereafter did him a favor in return by exercising their authority over the St. Lawrence project.

This is a fundamental phenomenon in policy making: Where A lacks authority over B, he will use his authority elsewhere to achieve an influence on B.

Because many policy issues come to be woven together in a play of power, authority in the hands of a policy maker in one field can typically be used to get some leverage in many other policy fields in which he lacks authority. A mayor may lack authority on educational policy in the primary and secondary schools. But if he has authority on the use of municipally owned land available for new school buildings, he can greatly influence educational policy. These multifold possibilities of exploiting authority in extended areas enormously complicate cooperation for policy making, for they permit large numbers of policy makers to intervene on any one policy issue. They compel a policy maker to submit to other policy makers on issues on which he does not acknowledge the legitimacy of their intervention. They also permit *ad hoc* interventions—even raids—for they permit a policy maker without continuing responsibility in a field to intervene and withdraw at will.

Exploiting one's authority indirectly in this way opens up endless possibilities for influencing other participants in the play of power. Political scientists have no standard list of the possibilities, so many and varied are they; but, clearly, participants differ greatly in their perception and exploitation of these possibilities. Knowing how to exploit them is, in fact, a large part of a politician's skill.

One of the major possibilities, however, is the use of one's legal authority indirectly to establish a new extra-legal authority. A student of politics has written about southern governors:

> It is fairly standard practice now for executive leaders to make a careful tabulation of legislative votes on gubernatorial programs and to tell dissenting legislators that, if attitudes and votes are not changed, they will get no more jobs for constituents, no more state-aid for rural roads in their districts, no more of the favors that are the lifeblood of state legislators. This relationship is not subtle; it is direct, brutal; and it is effective. Executive politicians now can—and do—back recalcitrant legislators against the wall and read the "riot act" to them.[12]

[12] D. Lockard, *The Politics of State and Local Government* (New York: The Macmillan Company, 1963), p. 372.

The Play in Main Outline

The governors use their legal authority over expenditures and jobs not simply to intervene *ad hoc* into legislative policy making but to induce legislators to accept an extra-legal rule of cooperation with the governors—to concede, specifically, an extra-legal authority to the governors.

Persuasion, Authority, and Money

We are often tempted to think that when one proximate policy maker wants to control another by other than persuasion, he has many different powers or sources of influence at his disposal. Almost always they rest on authority. If, for example, the President uses patronage to reward friends and punish enemies in order to bring congressmen around to his wishes, his power over them rests on his authority to hire and fire. The same is true for an official's use of public funds to win voters or colleagues; he can use them only because he has authority over funds. Doing favors for other proximate policy makers, or refusing to do them—both being typical instruments of power in politics— are usually possible only because one has authority to do or not to do.

What of the threat of violence as a source of power? Except for persons with authority to arrest, constrain, or execute, the attempt to exercise power through a threat of violence is illegal. It is not much used in policy making in democratic systems, not even much used in the administration of policy except against a fringe group of persons willing to consider breaking the law. Gunmen and gangsters use it to control other people, but policy makers do not.

MONEY IN POLICY MAKING

Does the role of money in policy making argue against the emphasis we have given to persuasion and authority? Rather than evoke, with anecdote and innuendo, an impression of a sinister influence, let us see if we can systematically describe the admittedly large role of wealth in policy making.

Money can hire printing presses, propagandists, policy analysts, and doorbell ringers. It is first, then, a prodigious influence in policy making because people and corporations with money can organize and support persuasion. We shall see in a later chapter that interest groups disproportionately represent people and corporations that can afford to meet the costs of organized persuasion. Parties too spend heavily for staff, travel, radio and television time, printed propaganda, and research. Anyone wealthy enough to make an exceptionally large contribution to the expenses of these methods of persuasion can gain some voice in the making of party policy, even more so in local and state party organizations.[13]

Beyond persuasion, the power of wealth requires closer analysis. Aside from persuasion, what can a man do to influence other men unless he has authority over them? He can hold out threats of punishment or promises of rewards in order to induce them to do as he wishes.

Generally, however, men are not allowed to threaten each other or to inflict injury on each other. As a method of influencing policy, threats therefore largely take a restricted form: someone in the policy-making system

[13] See A. Heard, *The Costs of Democracy* (Chapel Hill, N. C.: University of North Carolina Press, 1960), and A. Heard, *Money and Politics* (New York: Public Affairs Committee, Inc., 1956).

The Play in Main Outline

threatens not to behave cooperatively; a campaign contributor threatens to stop contributing or a senator threatens not to go along with party leadership; or—authority again—someone who has authority threatens to use it to make difficulties for other participants.

Reward is a horse of a different color. If I cannot injure my neighbor, I can reward him. Specifically, I enjoy wide freedom to pay money to him—in exchange for all kinds of things I might want from him. Money is the most far-reaching and manipulable of all devices for rewarding persons for doing what one wants of them.

So powerful is money in inducing men to do all manner of things that the rules of every political system restrict its use in policy making. In most governments, the formal rules—and in many governments, the effective rules—go far to prohibit any person from paying another person to make political decisions one way rather than another. It is legal to pay a man to do what one wants him to do if he is an employee of a firm or a supplier of market goods and services. But it is illegal to buy a vote, to buy a favorable decision from a judge, and to buy a legislator's or administrator's decision. In the U.S., the U.K., and the U.S.S.R. alike, paying for political favors, though not wholly suppressed, is driven underground; and the systematic routine use of money to buy favorable policies is, though nowhere to be proved, probably limited to less developed countries like Mexico.

That is not quite the end of the story, however. Because wealthy people do enjoy a "power" to reward other people, little restricted except in political life, they are in many societies objects of deference, if not of outright concessions of informal authority. Some people are strongly disposed to accept leadership from the wealthy; and many people allow themselves to be influenced by the legal or borderline favors that the wealthy can offer, almost without thinking, to those about them. Some congressmen, for example, find it difficult to refuse free airplane trips, the loan of automobiles, and the pleasures of dinner parties and weekends with the wealthy and with the managers of wealthy business enterprises. If, under these circumstances, the legal and informal rules of American politics prohibit an explicit exchange of favor for favor, it will nevertheless happen that a policy maker will feel a more solicitous concern for the wealthy than if he had not come to be counted among their friends.[14]

In short, money plays a big role in policy making, largely, we see, through its financing of political persuasion, but not entirely so. We might add that since wealth is distributed and employed according to man-made rules, its role in politics further illustrates the dependence of the play of power on rules.

Policy Analysis and the Structure of Rules

THE APPLECART

In a play of power governed by rules, some of the most perceptive participants in policy making come to understand that some kinds of policies would threaten to upset habitual rule observance. Changing the American system over to Cabinet government with a strong Prime Minister, for example, would

[14] Key, *Politics, Parties and Pressure Groups*, pp. 563ff.

threaten to render a network of existing rules obsolete, at the same time creating uncertainty as to what formal *and informal* rules would be needed to take their place, and even greater uncertainty as to whether the needed new rules would in fact come to be habitually accepted. Other participants in policy making, whether perceiving such a danger or not, are simply indoctrinated—by family training, elementary education, and other tradition-perpetuating institutions—not to question the main structure of rules, and to limit their consideration of policy to small changes.

Participants in the play of power also come to see that drastic changes in policy, even if not in the rules of the game themselves, often threaten habitual rule obedience. For people follow rules only as long as they are not alarmed by the policies emerging from the policy-making system. Or participants simply see that drastic changes in policy, because they do not fall within the range of indoctrinated beliefs, are not worth attempting. They will stimulate little support, and a massive opposition, in any society attached by habitual rules and attitudes to a narrow range of new policy possibilities around the *status quo*. No skilled political leader will propose or support, for example, the nationalization of railroads in the United States, a policy already effected in many other countries with different political habits.

Moreover, the wide dispersion of participation in policy making specified by the rules not typical of modern, complex industrial societies makes simplistic and drastic policy change difficult. Even though in time of crisis key participants in policy making may agree on somewhat sweeping policy changes, a genuinely drastic and sweeping change in policy is usually possible only through the kind of transformation of the whole policy-making system (as in the Russian Revolution) that throws policy making into the hands of a cooperating new key group.

In short, for all these reasons, an established and stable play of power is an applecart that (a) would be upset by drastic and sweeping changes in policy and that (b) has to be upset in order to achieve such policy changes. Hence, the play of power typically achieves small or incremental steps rather than transformations. In the United States, we take small steps for granted.[15]

[15] Does this mean that policy making, because of its game-like character, has a pronounced conservative bias? In one sense, it does indeed. The policy-making process does not upset the basic social and political framework; instead it conserves it. In the more usual sense, however, policy-making in this style—sequential and incremental—is not necessarily conservative, for the successive incremental policy steps under some circumstances follow on each other rapidly. A society may therefore be altered more quickly through a succession of incremental moves than through fewer but more drastic policy moves. The more drastic moves are possible, for all the reasons given, only in rare cases, unless they are accompanied by a revolution in the policy-making process itself. But revolutions are not easy to bring off, and only a few succeed. Through its rapid sequences of incremental change, the United States, we noted in Chapter Four, is engaged in a permanent revolution.

Sometimes the position of the Negro is cited as evidence of the slowness of change achieved through a sequence of increments. The fact is that after the somewhat drastic changes in policy toward the Negro at the time of the Civil War, policy making proceeded for many years sequentially and incrementally to take away from the Negro some of the wartime gains. Thereafter for many decades, no large number and no important group of participants in policy making made any significant moves at all on policy toward the Negro. If there was a failure, as many of us would now say there was, it was not that a sequence of increments proved too slow or too modest, but that almost no policy makers were interested in any sequence at all. That being, until the 1940's, the

The Play in Main Outline

In the light of all this, some of the devices used for making the most of analysis take on new significance. We saw in Chapter Four that if analysis is both sequential and incremental, it gains in competence. We can now see that sequential and incremental analysis fits into the play of power in policy making.

The strategies for extending analysis in Chapter Four also suit the practitioner of partisan analysis. For the participant in the play of power who tries to persuade others and to clarify his own position through partisan analysis finds that a concentration on incremental moves (in a never-ending sequence) in policy making suits his purposes excellently. His problem is immediate policy—decisions on here-and-now alternatives before him—and not distant future or "best" policies.

Like the sequential and incremental strategies, the strategy of remedial analysis also turns out to be well suited to the practitioner of partisan analysis.[16] For every policy decision is later judged to be in part mistaken. Policy is never exactly on target—for all the reasons discussed in earlier chapters. Hence in the actual play of power, policy making is in large part a process of remedying past errors in policy.

We are now in a position to examine the play of power in more detail—to look further into its three major features: its cooperative character, its use of partisan analysis, and its reliance on rules and authority.

---

disposition of policy makers toward Negroes, one could doubt that there is any ground for believing that a more drastic policy proposal to improve the position of Negroes could have been effected at all. For further discussion on the possible conservatism of incremental policy making, see D. Braybrooke and C. E. Lindblom, *A Strategy of Decision* (New York: The Free Press, 1963), pp. 106ff.

[16] For further discussion of incremental policy making, see *Ibid.,* Part II.

The Play in Main Outline

The Citizen
as Policy Maker

What is the role of the ordinary citizen in the play
of power in policy making? If the citizen delegates the immediate
or proximate tasks of policy making to a variety of specialists,
what is there left for him to do?[1]

[1] Our answer pertains largely to his participation in state and national
politics, as does most of the analysis of this book. Where appropriate, we refer
to local politics; but the difference in scale of system and degree of propinquity
of citizens differs so greatly from town and city, on one hand, to state and nation,
on the other, that we shall not do justice to policy making in local government.

In Authoritarian and Democratic Regimes

Citizens vote in China and the Soviet Union, but not in free elections that can remove those in power. They demonstrate, but on cue from their leaders rather than to influence them. They participate in the work of political parties, but to implement policies rather than to make them. Even in these regimes, however, the desires of ordinary citizens are consequential for policies chosen by those in power. Even an old-style military dictator will pay some minimum of attention to what his subjects want in order to keep down dangerous unrest.

The new breed of authoritarian ruler pursuing industrialization, economic power, and modernization has a second reason for attending to the wants and needs of the populace. People are resources whose productivity needs to be developed no less than the productivity of the nation's land and capital equipment. They need to be well fed, trained, motivated, even made proud; hence policy making has to attend to them.[2] It is not surprising that the Soviet Union gives university and postgraduate training to a greater proportion of its citizens than does Britain. Or that decades ago it pushed ahead of the United States in subsidized and free medical care.

A third channel of citizen influence on policy making in authoritarian regimes has been through the widespread acceptance by leaders of the *rule* that policy should give citizens a good deal of what they want even if citizens are not allowed to participate directly in the making of policy. Hence, Soviet ambition to out-perform the Western nations, especially the United States, in the level of consumer benefits to be given every citizen.[3]

The democracies offer, of course, opportunities for citizen participation denied in authoritarian regimes. Yet the first noteworthy fact about citizen participation in democratic policy making is that it is thin. Most citizens are little interested in playing even a small policy-making role; fully a third of American citizens neither vote, join interest groups, do party work, communicate with their representatives, nor talk politics with their friends (except occasionally in a vague and uninformed way). The table on page 45 shows the pattern.

As might be expected, people who care about the results appear to participate more than others.[4] The more educated are more active.[5] A University of Michigan Research Center study found that "many people who have limited familiarity with broad policy questions disenfranchise themselves." Conversely, high rates of participation go with high familiarity with issues.[6] Let us look into specific forms of participation.

[2] R. T. Holt and J. E. Turner (eds.), *Soviet Union: Paradox and Change* (New York: Holt, Rinehart and Winston, Inc., 1962), pp. 220*ff.*

[3] Documented in H. G. Shaffer (ed.), *The Soviet System* (New York: Appleton-Century-Crofts, 1965), pp. 263*ff.*

[4] A. Campbell, P. E. Converse, W. E. Miller, and D. E. Stokes, *The American Voter* (New York: John Wiley and Sons, Inc., 1960), p. 104.

[5] F. I. Greenstein, *The American Party System and the American People,* Foundations of Modern Political Science Series (Englewood Cliffs, N. J.: Prentice-Hall, Inc., 1963), p. 19.

[6] V. O. Key, Jr., *Public Opinion and American Democracy* (New York: Alfred A. Knopf, 1961), p. 185.

The Citizen as Policy Maker

Holding public and party office	Less
Being a candidate for office	than
Soliciting political funds	1%
Attending a caucus or a strategy meeting	
Becoming an active member of a political party	4–5%
Contributing time in a political campaign	
Attending a political meeting or rally	
Making a monetary contribution to a party or candidate	10%
Contacting a public official or a political leader	13%
Wearing a button or putting a sticker on the car	15%
Attempting to talk another into voting a certain way	25–30%
Initiating a political discussion	
Voting	
Exposing oneself to political stimuli	40–70%†

* Adapted from L. W. Milbrath, *Political Participation* (Chicago: Rand McNally & Co., 1965), pp. 18f.

† For 1960 as an illustrative year, Roper calculated that about 20 million out of 104 million "eligibles" were prevented from voting by residential requirements, illness, travelling, residence in the District of Columbia, barriers to Negroes, etc. Of the remaining eligibles, 80 per cent voted. (Elmo Roper, "How to Lose Your Vote," 44 *Saturday Review* (March 18, 1961).

Voting in Elections

The most conspicuous difference between authoritarian and democratic regimes is that in democratic regimes citizens choose their top policy makers in genuine elections.[7] Some political scientists speculate that voting in genuine elections may be an important method of citizen influence on policy not so much because it actually permits citizens to choose their officials and to some degree instruct these officials on policy but because the existence of genuine elections put a stamp of approval on citizen participation. Indirectly, therefore, the fact of elections enforces on proximate policy makers a moral rule that citizens' wishes count in policy making. The general rule that citizen interests should be respected in policy making is given special force by the fact of genuine elections, irrespective of whether and how citizens actually cast their votes.

Presumably there is something to this argument, even if the techniques

[7] If there is one most clear example of the dependence of power on rules, it is that of voting. Rules prescribe who can vote and how their votes are to be counted and weighed; and a rule prescribes that candidates declared to be winners take office as proximate policy makers. From government to government the content and effect of the rules varies. The effective informal rules in some Southern states limit Negro voting, for example. Some rules, for instance, call for proportional representation; others do not. For a brief discussion of how different rules, even if all are democratic, lead to different results, see A. N. Dragnich and J. C. Wahlke (eds.), *Government and Politics* (New York: Random House, 1961), pp. 434ff. See also D. Rae, *The Political Consequences of Electoral Laws* (New Haven: Yale University Press, 1967).

45

of contemporary political science are not sufficient to bring it down out of the realm of speculation. Beyond it, however, what can we say about the significance of actual voting for giving citizens an influence in the play of power?

In a few American states (California, for example) and a few countries (Switzerland, for example) citizens act on a significant amount of legislation by voting directly on it, and in many American states constitutional amendments come directly before the voters.[8] But direct participation in policy decisions through voting is impossible for all but a few decisions. There are simply too many decisions to be made. Even one difficult policy decision may run beyond the time and competence that the citizen can bring to it; and if there are thousands of decisions to be made, even simple ones cannot be decided by the vote. Each U. S. Congress passes between 600 and 1,000 bills, and turns down thousands more.

If voting is consequently typically limited to citizen choice of candidate for office rather than choice among policies, to what extent does voting give the citizen any kind of effective role in policy making?

ALTERNATIVE FUNCTIONS OF VOTING

It is not obvious that the vote is a significant instrument of citizen participation in the shaping of policy. For although a citizen may be able to use his vote to influence policies, he may not choose to do so. Some citizens wish to abdicate, not participate. They welcome the opportunity to turn policy making over to proximate policy makers and other leaders. Though voting, they cast their vote for a "good" man without respect to his policies, not even taking the trouble to ascertain them. [9]

Most people today shrink from believing that the vote is not an effective instrument of citizen policy making, for such a conclusion would seem to strike at democratic beliefs. But the vote is a valuable piece of the machinery of democracy even if it is not an instrument of citizen policy making, so that we can afford to look at it open-eyed, without prejudging its efficacy for citizen policy making.

Instead of constituting a general influence on policy, voting may serve such restricted, though critical, functions as:

Protecting personal liberties. A general invasion of traditional liberties, short of suppressing elections themselves, would presumably stimulate a sharp adverse reaction from voters. If habits of thought and action among officials account in part from solicitousness about personal liberties, it may also be that the threat of being turned out of office by the voters is also powerful.

Protecting democracy. Voting may be significant not as a method of influencing specific policy decisions but simply as an alternative (called "democracy") to recruitment of proximate policy makers by inheritance, by lot or rotation, or by consultation and maneuvering among a self-perpetuating oligarchy, as in the U.S.S.R. To be sure, selection of proximate policy makers by citizens carries some limited implications for policy, for policy

---

[8] For a summary of experience here and abroad with direct legislation, see A. Ranney and W. Kendall, *Democracy and the American Party System* (New York: Harcourt, Brace and World, Inc., 1956), Ch. 4.

[9] A. Campbell, P. E. Converse, W. E. Miller, and D. E. Stokes, *Elections and the Political Order* (New York: John Wiley and Sons, Inc., 1966), p. 207.

The Citizen as Policy Maker

makers so chosen will presumably pursue policies different from those of a nominee of oligarchs.

Energizing proximate policy makers. In traditional despotisms a chronic problem has often been the inactivity of political leadership. In many transitional societies, like those of Latin America, Vietnam, and India, leadership is still not sufficiently motivated to attack its problems.[10] Even with India's enthusiastic commitment to planned economic development, the civil service is still not oriented to problem solving as much as to its traditional law-and-order functions; and top leadership has often been more concerned with keeping the peace among conflicting language, caste, ethnic, regional, and other political groups than with employing public policy for any positive purposes.[11] Under such circumstances, elections may create a pressure to act, to solve problems, even if they do not give guidance on policies.

ONE VOTE: MANY POLICIES

An obstacle to making the vote generally an effective instrument of influence on specific policy issues is that the citizen has one vote while issues are many. If I agree with candidate Smith on 15 issues out of the 25 on which he has declared his position, and I agree with his rival McNally on the remaining 10, how can my single vote for Smith tell him on which issues I agree? I may even vote for Smith when I agree with McNally on most issues and with Smith on but one or a few, if that one or a few are more important to me than the many issues on which I agree with McNally; but, again, my vote fails to communicate anything to the winning candidate about what I wish on any of the issues. President Truman claimed a mandate to repeal the Taft-Hartley Act because he campaigned on a promise to do so. He had no such mandate, however, for he was elected by voters who endorsed him for reasons other than his position on Taft-Hartley, and it may even be that an overwhelming number of his supporters opposed his position on Taft-Hartley.

THE ROLE OF PARTIES

What has just been described is an obstacle to citizen influence on decisions on specific issues even if candidates' positions are clearly identified on each possible policy issue. Further obstacles—to be documented in the next chapter—are that candidates do not declare themselves at all on most policy issues, declare themselves ambiguously on others, and are not listened to by most voters anyway, with the result that most citizens vote either without caring much about their candidate's position on specific issues, or with a grossly distorted picture of what their candidate actually does stand for. Whether there is any connection between votes for a candidate and his position on policy issues is a difficult question which should be answered with caution.

Clearly, however, whether voters achieve an influence over specific policies will depend on how campaign issues are formulated, how candidates are or are not tied to specific policy positions, and on whether voters know the

[10] Motivational problems of leadership in Latin-American policy making on economic development are discussed in A. Hirschman, *Journeys Toward Progress* (New York: Twentieth Century Fund, 1963).

[11] A. H. Hanson, *The Process of Planning* (London: Oxford University Press, 1966), Ch. 7.

policy positions of candidates. If these matters were in the candidates' hands, whether the citizen could influence policy choices would vary from one candidate to another. To a degree it does vary in that way. In almost all democratic political systems, however, candidates belong to political parties. How issues are formulated and whether candidates commit themselves to policy positions depend therefore largely on the character of the party system. To pursue further the question of the importance of voting as a method of policy participation thus requires a study of the electoral role of political parties. We will turn to it in the next chapter.

THE NON-VOTER

Viewing the vote as a method of citizen participation, one should not feel that the non-voter has withdrawn from the policy-making system. He may or may not have done so. Some non-voters are not at all apathetic; they may abstain only because satisfied with what government is doing—and stand ready to intervene with their votes at any time they become dissatisfied. Many non-voters in off-year congressional elections become voters in Presidential elections, in which they think the stakes are higher; and in other ways big issues pull to the polls persons who are usually among the non-voters, as is shown by a strong tendency for pre-war elections to draw more heavily than post-war.[12] And some citizens, we noted, disenfranchise themselves in favor of better-informed voters. Yet perhaps a million and a half Negroes are in one way or another prevented from voting. And millions more Negroes and other citizens like the Mexicans in the Southwest, the Puerto Ricans, and the native uneducated poor, are deprived of the vote by their degree of ostracism from the political community. Voters vote not because they carefully calculate the advantage of so doing; they are indoctrinated from birth with dispositions to vote, just as some of them pick up attitudes and dispositions that lead them to organize or otherwise exert themselves in policy making. Millions of American citizens are not socialized in this way; they do not have the habit of political participation, are not encouraged to pick up such a habit, and are isolated from those who might show them how and why to participate. They are members of subcultures that do not teach the values or the methods of political participation.[13]

Other Forms of Citizen Policy Making in Democracies

PARTY WORK

Beyond voting are other possibilities of citizen participation in the play of power in policy making. Although we are postponing to another chapter the question of whether and how political parties raise the effectiveness of the vote as a form of participation, we can here ask whether actual participation in party work is an important avenue of citizen participation in policy making. Quantitatively, the answer is clear. At the most, only about 5 to 7

[12] Greenstein, *The American Party System and the American People*, p. 10; and R. E. Lane, *Political Life* (Glencoe, Ill.: The Free Press, 1959), p. 26.

[13] For a survey of what we know about failures in socialization (as well as other factors) in political participation, see Milbrath, *Political Participation*. For discussion of alternative patterns of socialization, see G. A. Almond and G. B. Powell, Jr., *Comparative Politics* (Boston: Little, Brown & Co., 1966), Ch. 3.

48

per cent of Americans are in any way active in party work, and only about 10 per cent go so far as to contribute money to a political party.[14] The overwhelming majority do not even try to participate.

What about the small number who do? Some are hardly ordinary citizens. They are political leaders of various kinds. Some of them are not interested in policy, but in a job through patronage. Or they like the sociability of party work, the wide circle of friends they can claim, or the opportunity to do favors. It is probably safe to say that most party workers are in the party for reasons other than promoting policies they prefer.[15]

COLLECTION, DISCUSSION, AND COMMUNICATION OF INFORMATION ON POLICY

Policy, we have seen, is responsive to information, discussion, and study, especially to partisan analysis. Do ordinary citizens effectively participate in these activities?

A citizen can write or talk to his congressman to tell him what he wants or needs, or thinks ought to be done about a problem. But, as we have seen, only about 10 or 15 per cent of Americans do so, and then only rarely. A citizen can informally take part in the never-ending discussion among citizens about public affairs, an exchange of views that unquestionably influences proximate policy makers because they are informed by their own participation in it. But, as we have seen, perhaps no more than one in five Americans sees himself as participating in discussion with his friends and neighbors on public affairs; and the number who add anything to what has already been said is much smaller.[16]

PARTICIPATION IN INTEREST GROUPS

For all but a few citizens, fact gathering and analysis is ineffective without organization. If a citizen wants to be an effective influence on policy and is not, as a scholar or journalist, strategically placed to make an individual contribution to analysis, he has to join forces with other citizens. Only with others can he hire the specialized services of researcher, attorney, lobbyist, or whoever else is needed to influence policy. At the same time, organization opens up the possibility of his communicating with his fellow citizens to see whether they can agree on policies to be sought, and to use the promise of their massed vote to influence elected officials or to choose new ones. Perhaps a third of Americans are in some way affiliated with such organizations.

Millions of citizens, however, join such groups for reasons removed from policy making. Trade union members join unions largely for nonpolitical reasons—for higher wages, for job security, or because all their fellows in the plant are members. In an interesting recent study, Mancur Olson presented argument and evidence that the typical situation is that members are attached to interest groups by group services (the American Medical Association, for example, helps in defense against malpractice suits) rather than by the policy-making activity of the group.[17]

[14] T. R. Dye, *Politics, Economics, and the Public* (Chicago: Rand McNally & Co., 1966), p. 59.

[15] Ranney and Kendall, *Democracy and the American Party System*, pp. 241f.

[16] See also J. L. Woodward and E. Roper, "Political Activity of American Citizens," 44 *American Political Science Review* (December, 1950), p. 874.

[17] *The Logic of Collective Action* (Cambridge: Harvard University Press, 1965), especially Ch. 6.

The Citizen as Policy Maker

Then, too, insofar as the citizen affiliates with an interest group because of its policy activity he may turn to it less as a method of influencing policy than as *another device for delegation of the task of policy making.* Not content with simply delegating proximate policy making to officials, he wants also to delegate the task of watching and influencing them. He is active only in making a financial contribution or in registering himself as a member.

Just what citizen influence actually amounts to through interest group organization will depend on two things: (a) how the interest-group leaders influence policy, and (b) how the citizen relates to the interest-group leaders. These will have to be topics for later chapters on interest groups and on the interconnections among all participants in the play of power.

Disobedience or Civil Disorder

In the inter-war years, one French premier after another had trembled before, or was displaced because of the agitation of, Parisian mobs. In 1966, Indian Prime Minister Gandhi and her Cabinet surrendered to the demands of rioters asking for new legal bans on cow slaughter. And in the United States in the late sixties, mayors, governors, and the President were desperate to find policies that would put an end to what appeared to be an emerging cycle of summer rioting in the cities. Civil disobedience appears to be an effective method of citizen participation in the play of power in policy making.

Why should the rioting, looting, and violence of tiny minorities—and, sometimes, legal demonstrations that only hint at disobedience—so frighten proximate policy makers? Because they create a dilemma in democratic government. If the disobedience is severe enough, it can be suppressed only by repressive measures hostile to liberty and democracy, as we saw in the summer of 1967 when National Guardsmen in New Jersey invaded Negro homes to search indiscriminately for weapons. If not suppressed, it is contagious to a degree that threatens orderly government. Why? Because the rules and authority on which democratic government rests are for the most part either voluntarily accepted, or enforced in relatively non-coercive ways by the many who do voluntarily accept them. They are not typically enforced by police or army.

When a substantial number of citizens disavow rules and authority, they break the habit of obedience without which orderly democratic government is impossible. They also show how easy it is to do so. They reveal that very little coercion usually lies behind rules and authority. And they, by their own change of attitude, reduce significantly the ranks of those who, through rebuke and various forms of ostracism, hold the potentially disobedient in check. In a new and troubled democracy like India, no leader ever knows when a localized disobedience will wildly spread and bring down the regime.

For these reasons, disobedience is as powerful as it is. It is not more powerful because, like an atomic bomb used in Vietnam, it could trigger such a terrible reaction that responsible men dare not use it. In an unstable system, disobedience is most effective in the hands of groups who are more interested in coup or revolution than in specific policy changes. In a stable system, it it most effective in the hands of persons whose demands are so deeply felt that they are willing to suffer both potentially serious penalties to themselves, and unknown destabilizing consequences for the whole political system—as indeed some American Negroes have now decided to do.

Subtler forms of disobedience are sometimes an effective instrument for citizen participation in policy making. Tax evasion, for example, ties the hands of proximate policy makers. In many underdeveloped countries, proximate policy makers can achieve only the loosest control over tax policy. They can neither raise the funds required for public purposes, including economic development, nor control the distribution of the tax burden on the citizenry. An obvious defect of this and related forms of disobedience is, of course, that the citizens thereby frustrate policy making not only by the proximate policy makers but by everyone and anyone. Tax evasion throws away tax policy as an effective instrument; no one can use it.

Citizen Competence

Insofar as the citizen does participate in policy making, what information does he have and what efforts does he make to inform himself? And how does he conceive of, analyze, or understand political issues?

A University of Michigan Survey Research Center study of a sample of citizens divided them into two groups: those who had no opinion on representative policy issues, and those who did. Among those who did, the study then tried to weed out uninformed opinions by ascertaining whether expressed opinion was related to any knowledge of government policies. The upshot of the study was that two-thirds of the sample of citizens knew at least something about representative issues and were sufficiently concerned to be able to voice an opinion. It was not a picture of comprehensive ignorance. On the other hand, the two-thirds who had an opinion and some knowledge are not to be understood as well informed; they only "knew something," which often was not much.[18]

Researchers in the same organization tried a somewhat different inquiry into the level of information and understanding of voters by ascertaining how voters formulated issues. Did voters relate their vote to an organized set of ideas or principles? Or to benefits to groups of which they considered themselves to be members? Or could they only make vague references, in explaining their votes, to phenomena like war, recession, or prosperity—to the nature of the times? Or was their vote related to no issue at all—perhaps to habit, or personality trait of voter or candidate?

> For:
> 15½ per cent of voters, the vote was related to an organized set of ideas;
> 45 per cent, the vote was related to group benefits;
> 23 per cent, the vote was related vaguely to the nature of the times;
> 17½ per cent, the vote seemed unrelated to any public issues.[19]

What citizens know depends of course on how they gather information. The evidence is that they give little energy to the task. Of a sample of people interviewed after the 1956 presidential campaign:

[18] Campbell, *et al., The American Voter*, p. 174.
[19] *Ibid.*, p. 249.

69 per cent read about the campaign in newspapers
45 per cent listened to radio speeches or discussion
74 per cent watched campaign programs on television
31 per cent read about the campaign in magazines[20]

If that sample is at all representative, the percentages might be taken to mean that a large proportion of the population in the United States takes the trouble to inform itself at least in a case of a presidential election. To what extent, however, do they gather significant information from these sources? In the sample referred to, the 69 per cent who read about the campaign in newspapers included anyone who had read anything in any newspaper. Some idea of how some people read news about public affairs is given us from another sample of persons who were asked how they read national and international news.[21] They responded:

Do not read news	4%
Just headlines, skim	47
More than headlines, not much	4
Sometimes carefully, sometimes not	14
Carefully, skip some things	19
Very carefully	6
National carefully, international not	3
International carefully, national not	1
Not ascertained	2

If we put these two pieces of information together—that many people read about a campaign in newspapers but that reading usually means skimming the headlines—we see that the flow of communication on public affairs from the media to the citizen is extremely thin. If the mass media barrage the citizen with communications, little of it is on politics, and only a small part of that gets through to the citizen. We shall look into this question further in several other chapters.

So far, the picture is one of little citizen influence in policy making and of poorly informed and happenstance influence at that. Everything said so far, however, has to be considered as preliminary and inconclusive until we can look further into the electoral role of parties and into interest groups, both in the U. S. and abroad, as we shall now do. We shall see that citizen influence is more significant than at this point it appears to be.

[20] Key, *Public Opinion and American Democracy*, p. 346.
[21] *Ibid.*, p. 352.

The Citizen as Policy Maker

The Voter
and Party
Competition

CHAPTER SEVEN

It does not look as though the ballot is an effective instrument
of citizen participation in the play of power in policy
making. Many citizens do not vote. And of those who do, most know
little—and much of what they know is mistaken—about specific
policies for which competing candidates stand.
A study of voters in congressional elections showed that
46 per cent of those voting alleged that they did so without
hearing or reading anything about the candidates
(they simply voted by party); and those

53

voters who did hear or read something evaluated candidates by personality, experience, and presumed general competence; rarely by reference to any policy issue.[1]

Tying Candidates to Policy Positions

Yet through political parties, voters do in fact achieve a significant influence on policy—a modest, limited influence, to be sure, but larger than might so far be expected.[2] A simple explanation, later to be qualified, begins this way: In two-party systems, parties formulate policy issues to which candidates of the party are to some degree tied. The significance of the tie is that the voter can exert a general influence on policy by supporting candidates of that party whose general policy inclinations or specific commitments are attractive to him. He can choose one or another party's package of policy more confidently than he can pick and choose among a large number of candidates and policies.

TIGHT AND LOOSE TIES

In a political system like the British, in which national party officials control the selection of candidates and can refuse party standing to elected officials who no longer remain loyal to party directives, candidates can be conspicuously and securely tied to a party platform, so that the voter knows, if he takes the trouble to familiarize himself with party declarations, what each candidate stands for. He need know nothing about the candidate other than his party affiliation.[3]

In the American system, in which parties commit themselves vaguely on policy issues and in which candidates are relatively free, both during the campaign and after election, to disavow the party platform, the tie between party and policy issues is weaker.[4] But it is still there. In some American states, party discipline actually holds legislators to a position as firmly as in

[1] A. Campbell, P. E. Converse, W. E. Miller, and D. E. Stokes, *Elections and the Political Order* (New York: John Wiley and Sons, Inc., 1966), pp. 204ff.

[2] Parties play their part in policy making according to legal and extra-legal rules that have, in democratic regimes, sprung from widespread appreciation among political activists of the usefulness of party organization. Thus, for example, in the United States the extra-legal rule has developed, superimposed on constitutional rules for voting in the electoral college, that electors should cast their vote for President not at their own discretion but according to party affiliation. One of the problems of modernizing countries is to find rules on which the parties can agree as the condition for orderly government.

[3] For more on British parties, see R. T. McKenzie, *British Political Parties* (New York: Frederick A. Praeger, 1964).

[4] That on this score the British system gives citizens a more certain control over policy than does the American system is a significant fact, but no one should rush to conclude that it is an advantage of the British system. Whether it is is a difficult question. This chapter offers some ground for an answer. For the moment, we say only that, depending on how uninformed and intransigent citizens are, their participation in policy making, as distinct from their participation in choosing policy makers, is sometimes to be regretted, even in the democracies. "The kind of issue that stimulates widespread participation in politics is also the kind of issue likely to create wide cleavages in society" (L. W. Milbrath, *Political Participation* [Chicago: Rand McNally & Co., 1965], p. 147). On policy issues, leaders are both more competent and more conciliatory than are citizens.

54

some of the European democracies. In national politics in the United States, party influence seems to be stronger than any other pressure on the legislators. Studies have confirmed what our common experience suggests; in one study, questionnaires returned by party leaders showed that Democratic leaders:

typically display the stronger urge to elevate the lowborn, the uneducated, the deprived minorities, and the poor in general. . . . They are more critical of wealth and big business and more eager to bring them under regulation. . . . The Republican leaders, while not uniformly differentiated from their opponents, subscribe in greater measure to the symbols and practices of individualism, *laissez-faire,* and national independence.[5]

Do voters in fact usually vote on party lines rather than by independent appraisal of candidates? Indeed they do, although, again, we shall later have to qualify the oversimplified answer to the question. Many Michigan Survey Research Center studies have shown that "No element of the political lives of Americans is more impressive than their party loyalties."[6] In one sample of voters, 80 per cent of adult citizens did not recall ever changing their party identification,[7] and a majority of those who identify with a party report that they have never deserted their party at an election.

The One Vote: Many Policies Problem

Even if, because parties tie candidates to policies, voters can influence policy generally, it is still the case, as we saw in the preceding chapter, that with one vote each they cannot pick and choose among various specific policies. They have to take the whole Republican basket or the whole Democratic basket. How does party competition help on this score?

To use again an oversimplified explanation later to be qualified: Where parties must compete to win elections, party leadership will be motivated to seek out information on citizen preferences beyond the inadequate information revealed to them by the ballot itself. In so doing they in effect give power over specific policies to citizens despite the fact that, for the reason just given, citizens cannot express their specific policy preferences in their vote.

On policy preferences that are clearly held by an overwhelming majority of citizens, ranging from protection of law and order, through honesty in government, to high-level employment and reasonable price stability, a political party would be suicidal not to satisfy them. The result is that on policy issues such as these, both parties join in offering the citizens what an overwhelming majority of them want—on each such specific policy. On each policy issue on which there is not a fairly clearly perceived overwhelming majority, each party will do its best to find a position that stands a good

---

[5] H. McClosky, P. J. Hoffmann, and R. O'Hara, "Issue Conflict and Consensus among Party Leaders and Followers," 54 *American Political Science Review* (June, 1960).

[6] Campbell, *et al., Elections and the Political Order,* p. 126.

[7] W. E. Miller, "Party Identification and Partisan Attitudes," in R. E. Wolfinger (ed.), *Readings in American Political Behavior,* Foundations of Modern Political Science Series (Englewood Cliffs, N.J.: Prentice-Hall, Inc., 1966), p. 249.

chance of appealing to a majority. It will want to avoid being caught on any one issue in a position on which it will offend more voters than it will gain.[8]

Voters will thus be offered by each party its idea of what it thinks a majority wants. Whichever version voters choose will give them approximately what they want on each policy issue. Differences between the alternative versions will be of secondary importance.

To see the full import of this conclusion, imagine that it were possible to induce parties to compete to win an election and then at the last moment cancel the election, choosing a winning party by toss of a coin. Would it matter which party won the toss? The greatest effect of the anticipated election would be to drive both parties to positions calculated to appeal to a majority. It would be the force of the anticipated election on party and candidate position that would give voters control over proximate policy makers and policy. In our hypothetical case, voters receive this benefit even if the election is cancelled at the last moment. What further and more precise control they achieve by choosing finally between the two parties, both of which are competing to satisfy the voters, is a secondary or smaller gain for the voter.[9]

It is often a source of complaint that the parties are alike as Tweedle-dee and Tweedle-dum. The complaint confirms our argument. If the two competing parties differed greatly in the platforms they offered to voters, it would mean that at least one of the parties had failed to approximate the preference of the majority and had blundered, therefore, into a set of policies that should have been rejected well before the campaign began. Those who say that one of the two major parties should have offered in the mid-sixties an unambiguous "withdraw from Vietnam" policy do not realize that neither party could afford to so long as it was clear that a majority would not support such a policy. Were such a policy thought capable of generating majority support, both parties would then have offered versions of it to the voter.

---

[8] In *An Economic Theory of Democracy* (New York: Harper and Brothers, 1957) Anthony Downs made a significant attempt to describe the process in formal theoretical terms, the theory based on axioms very much like those used in formal economic theory.

[9] In France, Italy, and many other countries, more than two parties engage in electoral campaigning; and normally no party expects to win a majority of the seats in the Parliament. Under these circumstances, party appeals to voters will be different from what we have described for two-party systems. For example, the parties may not try to find a collection of policies or issues that would appeal to a heterogeneous segment of voters, but instead may try to attract a group somewhat more homogeneous in attitude or policy disposition than a heterogeneous majority. They then expect their elected members to join a coalition of parties in the Parliament, with the number of their positions in the Cabinet (and the possibility of one of their members becoming Prime Minister) depending on the size of their party in the Parliament relative to the size of other parties.

A consequence is that, even with strict party discipline, the citizen is even more removed than in the two-party system from a direct choice among alternative collections of policies. The collections of policies that will prevail will not be worked out until the parliamentary coalition is formed after the election. And if we imagine the coalition "platform" as representing the majority's preferences, it is nevertheless a platform on which no voter has had an opportunity to cast a vote directly. For a summary of a variety of party systems, see G. M. Carter and J. H. Herz, *Government and Politics in the Twentieth Century* (New York: Frederick A. Praeger, 1965), Chs. 3 and 5.

The Voter and Party Competition

In short, simply to win elections two competing parties will:

1. seek information on specific policy preferences of voters;
2. disavow for each policy issue a large number of policy positions known or thought to be unacceptable to a majority of voters;
3. hence in effect make for voters a complicated set of choices that they could not make for themselves but that nevertheless respond to their preferences;
4. and thus present to the voters on election day itself only two packages of remaining policy positions, each package designed on each policy to appeal to a majority.[10]

Do voters actually hold the control over specific policies that the argument implies? How does the argument now need qualifying?

Majorities Control and Minorities Control of Policy

Sometimes a party can capture voters by taking a policy position that concerns some voters greatly—on which preferences are intense—better than by a position on a less deeply felt issue. In a controversy over routing a new highway, a local or state party might win more votes by favoring the wishes of a deeply disturbed and alert minority about to be evicted to make room for the highway than by endorsing the preference of an inattentive majority. The minority group will know what the party stands for and will vote. The majority may do neither.[11]

The possibility of intense minorities achieving an influence over policy does not damage the argument, as so far constructed, that party competition throws into the hands of ordinary voters a great deal of influence on specific policies—issue by issue. It does open up the possibility, however, that certain kinds of minorities rather than majorities will sometimes be in the driver's

[10] Many Americans live in municipalities in which party competition is ineffective; and many live in states in which competition within a party has to take the place, if anything does, of competition between parties. Until the Democratic dominance of the South began to break up, the Southern states were single-party states. Between 1929 and 1956, all the Southern states and Oklahoma had Democratic governors without exception. New Hampshire and Vermont had Republican governors exclusively. In some other states the domination of one party over the other was almost unbroken for the same period.

In these circumstances, factions within the parties take on some of the characteristics of parties; and just as there are two-party and multi-party regimes, so also there are bi-factional and multi-factional regimes.

Factional rivalry does not play quite the same role in policy making as does party rivalry. Factions lack continuity both in name and in actual structure. Hence the voter does not necessarily know to which faction a candidate belongs, nor if he knows at one date does he necessarily know at a later date. Effective competition between the factions is also weakened by the ease with which members can change from one faction to another. Persons and personalities become more critical, and issues less critical, to electoral success. In short, a vote for a candidate is even further disassociated from an expression of preference for any particular policy or collection of policies. See V. O. Key, Jr., *Southern Politics* (New York: Alfred A. Knopf, 1950), Ch. 14.

[11] An illuminating theoretical discussion of this possibility and of its implications for democratic theory is in R. A. Dahl, *A Preface to Democratic Theory* (Chicago: University of Chicago Press, 1956), Chs. 4 and 5.

The Voter and Party Competition

seat. In any case, we see that party platforms can respond significantly not merely to the presence or absence of a voter preference but to the intensity of that preference.

Voters Drawn to Party or Candidate other than by its Policies

A significant qualification to the line of argument taken on voter influence, both generally and on specific policies, is that voters are attracted to parties for reasons other than that the party offers them policies or dispositions they endorse.

Family affiliation. The evidence seems to indicate that voters are less attracted to a party by its stand than simply born into it. One study shows that among adults 70 to 80 per cent of offspring of active party members (where both parents are of the same party) will identify themselves as members of their parents' party, and 60 to 70 per cent of offspring of inactive party members will so identify themselves.[12] Most voters pick up their party loyalties while still in grammar school.

Other reference-group affiliations. Insofar as parental influence is not controlling, either in childhood or at a later period when the child or young adult breaks away from it, a new attachment to party may be picked up—without regard to party policies—from the groups with which the voter associates or to which he refers for political orientation: church, union, ethnic group, or social class, for example.[13]

Deliberate delegation. Many voters, we noted earlier, will deliberately refrain from choosing or rejecting a party by reference to its policies. They want to abdicate from policy making; they want their political leaders to do the job. Even more common is the voter who, if not attached to a party for family or other non-policy reasons, is attached to his party because he likes its position on those few policy issues on which he himself has a preference. On dozens or hundreds of other policy issues on which the party could declare or does declare itself, he abdicates. Many voters, we saw earlier, vote on the basis of diffused evaluative judgment on the candidate rather than his position on issues; they look for a "good man," or one who is experienced, or something of the sort.[14]

Misperception. Many voters so badly misperceive candidate and party position that, though they may vote by reference to policy issues, they vote for the wrong candidate or party.[15]

Party strategy. Finally, party leaders will often discourage voters from attaching to party on policy grounds. They will deliberately seek to attract voters with slogans, extremely general and abstract declarations, colorful leaders, and pageantry, avoiding a commitment on policy or policy disposition.

REMAINING SIGNIFICANCE OF APPEALS THROUGH POLICY

For all these reasons, then, party competition does not take the exclusive form of competitive party offers of attractive policies or policy dispositions. Yet that

[12] A. Campbell, P. E. Converse, W. E. Miller, and D. E. Stokes, *The American Voter* (New York: John Wiley and Sons, Inc., 1960), p. 147.

[13] *Ibid.*, Chs. 12 and 13.

[14] Campbell, *et al.*, *Elections and the Political Order*, p. 207.

[15] Campbell, *et al.*, *The American Voter*, p. 180.

The Voter and Party Competition

kind of competition, without which voters have almost no influence on specific policies, remains an important component of party competition. //

From the figures above, it is apparent that a third of voters do *not* vote as their parents did (and, of those who do, some may do so because they like their party's policies). And though most voters think of themselves as attached to a party, most of them have, at one time or another, voted against a candidate of their own party. Even the standpatters, those who never or rarely abandon their party, may stand pat not because they are indifferent to policy but because their party continues to satisfy them, year after year, on its policies or policy dispositions. "The standpatters of each party," V. O. Key, Jr., concluded after studying their voting behavior, "manifest fairly high agreement with the party positions as popularly perceived."[16]

On misperception of issues, if we have said—following one study—that 50 per cent of voters who have policy opinions cannot discriminate between parties, there is the other 50 per cent who can. If in the preceding chapter we showed that something under a half of voters had no opinion and knew nothing about what government was doing on a list of important policy issues, something over a half did have an opinion and did know something.

Threatened or actual swings of votes at the margin take on special significance. Even if *most* voters are rigid and irrational stand-patters, parties will be compelled to compete by offering attractive policies or policy dispositions, if there is a large enough margin of voters who care about issues to swing an election. In an American presidential election, a division of the vote of 55 per cent to 45 per cent is a landslide, and a 52–48 or 53–47 split is common. Thus, small changes at the margin in the pattern of votes cast throw the election one way or the other.

Does their responsiveness to party offers prove that swing voters alone achieve control over policy? The voters who swing in any given election are those whose usual party has recently disappointed them. For every one of them, there are presumably many more who might have swung but who did not because their party succeeded in making them an acceptable offer. And we have the evidence of Key's studies that even the standpatters—or at least many of them—stand ready to swing, and in fact stand pat only because the party succeeds year after year in suiting them. Assuming that parties are effective in ferreting out preferences and satisfying them for most citizens, we would expect to see only a small margin of voters actually swinging in any one election. And this is what we do see. What we see is consistent with the conclusion that parties respond to the influence or power of vastly greater numbers of citizens than the number actually defecting from their usual party in any one election.

SELECTIVE CONTROL OVER POLICY

// Not a single voter in any political system, however, has an opinion or preference on all the policy problems that will have to be decided after the election. We can say, consequently, that party competition on policy grounds can, because of marginal swings, give voters a powerful influence on some specific policies, but not on a multitude of them.// In 1968, swing voters could

---

[16] V. O. Key, Jr., *The Responsible Electorate* (Cambridge: Harvard University Press, 1966), p. 53.

The Voter and Party Competition

influence specific policy on Vietnam, race relations, and urban problems. On hundreds of issues on tax and fiscal policy, economic growth, foreign aid, transportation, relations with NATO, and education, however, voters could not be so effective.

It adds a little precision to our formulation of citizen participation in the play of power to say that *citizens shift their vote more because of the effects of policies than because of the policies themselves.* Elections are often lost by the party in power because a swing group is dissatisfied with what the party in power has accomplished.[17] In the 1953 Presidential campaign, many voters joined in turning out the Democratic Party because they reacted against the Korean war, some appearances of internal communism, and political corruption. Without quite knowing what specific policies the Republicans would inaugurate, voters chose a new slate of officials with a strong push to develop new policies on the three issues.

Other Qualifications

Parties that do not try to win. The argument that party competition gives citizens important influence in the play of power in policy making, both generally and on specific issues, rests, of course, on the assumption that parties do compete to win elections. Sometimes, however, party pursuit of other objectives takes priority over winning. Or, for institutional reasons, they will fail to compete with vigor. A party can develop institutional barriers to the pursuit of victory; it was widely believed, for example, that many local and state lower- and middle-level Republican Party leaders supported Goldwater for President in 1964 because his candidacy would strengthen their power in the party relative to the central national leadership of the party, and not because they thought he could win.

Lack of party solidarity. We will say once more, as a reminder, that party competition on policy can put policy-making power into the hands of the voter only to the extent that candidates follow the party position once elected. As we have noted, they do so in many European democracies and in some American states, but less so in most American states and in American national politics.

Incompetence in ascertaining citizen preferences. Finally, party competition on policy issues is effective in putting power over policy in the hands of the voter only to the degree that the parties do correctly ascertain voter preferences (on those issues in which voters actually have preferences) and thus succeed in making attractive alternative offers to voters.

Party Control over the Voter

The effect of parties is not simply to respond (or fail to respond) to voter preferences; it is also to form them. It becomes a major function of the opposition political parties, especially of their top leaders and their staffs, to carry on a running scrutiny of the party in power and to formulate coherent criticism and possible alternative policies for citizens. In addition to that kind of partisan analysis, they are also successful in a great amount of nonrational

[17] Campbell, *et al., The American Voter,* p. 554.

and irrational indoctrination. For citizens draw heavily on their chosen party as a reference group, like family, church, union, and other associations, for guidance on political attitudes and issues.

Summarizing their many voting studies, the authors of *The American Voter* raise the question: Does the voter pick a party to suit his attitudes, or pick his attitudes to suit his party? Their answer is unambiguous, even if their language is wooden:

. . . in the period of our studies the influence of party identification on attitudes toward creating these opinions by fixing the framework of public thinking about influence of these attitudes on party identification itself.[18]

In his prize-winning study of British politics, Samuel Beer writes:

"Party does not merely aggregate the opinions of groups, it goes a long way toward creating these opinions by fixing the framework of public thinking about policy and the voters' sense of the alternatives and the possibilities." He goes on to say that ". . . the parties themselves, backed by research staffs, equipped with nationwide organizations, and enjoying the continuous attention of the mass media, have themselves in great part framed and elicited the very demands to which they then respond."[19]

As we saw in an earlier chapter, the play of power is softened by the indoctrination of citizen and leader—by their consequent agreement on a code of fair play, on the rules of the political game, and on specific policy issues that would otherwise tear society apart. Political parties are among those social institutions and processes that accomplish such an integrating indoctrination in their efforts to form citizen attitudes and preferences.

Parties try to avoid making enemies. If their stands are consequently sometimes cowardly, evasive, or fuzzy, their influence is nevertheless to soften rather than exacerbate conflict among citizens and leaders. Party activity tends to push all participants in policy making away from intransigence on specific issues and programs, though at the same time permitting a rhetoric of intransigence. Moreover, parties are also highly motivated to teach citizens the difference between the preferred and the possible, and no lesson is more powerful than that in moderating citizen demands and reducing the range of disagreement. We shall have more to say about this in Chapter Twelve.

[18] *Ibid.*, p. 135.
[19] S. H. Beer, *British Politics in the Collectivist Age* (New York: Alfred A. Knopf, 1966), p. 347.

Interest-Group Leaders

Whatever their oft-criticized sins, interest groups—most
of us concede—help citizens decide what they want,
and call their desires to the attention of proximate policy makers.
In some political science circles it has become common to say
that the "articulation of interests" is in fact the distinctive
function of these groups.[1]

[1] G. A. Almond and G. B. Powell, Jr., for example, in *Comparative
Politics* (Boston: Little, Brown & Co., 1966), pp. 74*ff*.

Superficial opinions to the contrary, the interests they articulate are not always self-serving. Many groups pursue versions of the "public interest"—for example, the League of Women Voters, or the groups designed to influence policy on Vietnam. Many other groups pursue specific narrow interests, but not the interests of the members, except for their interest in the welfare of others or their interest in political action itself. As E. E. Schattschneider has said, the members of the American League to Abolish Capital Punishment obviously do not expect to be hanged.[2]

How They Influence Policy

It is the proximate policy maker, not the interest-group leader, who has the actual authority to make policy. If interest-group leaders communicate their desires to a proximate policy maker, it is not at all clear why the latter pays any attention. Why does he?

MOBILIZATION OF THE VOTE

Perhaps the most common pertinent opinion in the United States is that interest groups are powerful because their members are voters. Many political scientists doubt the adequacy of this explanation, however; and V. O. Key, Jr., has persuasively argued that if interest groups try to threaten a public official with their claims to control votes, "they are usually pointing an unloaded gun at the legislator."[3]

By no means do Key and others argue that group affiliations do not affect the vote. The argument is instead that group affiliations are a relatively stable element in a citizen's disposition to vote one way or the other, and that an interest-group leader is simply not successful in inducing a *change* in vote to reward or punish a public official. To tie a group to a party requires a cumbersome process of indoctrination. Once achieved, the tie between group and party is not easily then manipulated. The party has simply captured the group more or less permanently.[4]

For other reasons too, the interest group finds it difficult to "deliver the vote":

1. Many interest groups are too small to count.

2. In the heterogeneous mass-interest groups (like trade unions) that contain enough voters to count, some members vote as trade unionists, some as Catholics, some as conservatives, some as liberals, some as farmers (because of their origins), and so on.

3. In these mass organizations, leadership does not communicate effectively with the rank and file. One survey showed that only 28 per cent of union members and 20 per cent of members of farm organizations had ever received any literature from their organizations about candidates for public office.[5]

[2] E. E. Schattschneider, *The Semi-Sovereign People* (New York: Holt, Rinehart and Winston, Inc., 1960), p. 26.

[3] V. O. Key, Jr., *Public Opinion and American Democracy* (New York: Alfred A. Knopf, 1961), p. 522.

[4] On how such a tying process often works, see A. Campbell, P. E. Converse, W. E. Miller, and D. E. Stokes, *The American Voter* (New York: John Wiley and Sons, Inc., 1960), pp. 327*ff*.

[5] Key, *Public Opinion and American Democracy*, p. 522.

4. As we shall shortly see, interest-group leaders typically seek a lasting relation of confidence with the proximate policy maker. Consequently, they cannot threaten. Even if he offends them on a specific policy, they want to maintain good relations in order to influence him in the future.

5. As is consistent with what we saw of voter behavior in the preceding chapter, attachment to party or candidate overrides attachment to particular issues in an election.

6. In Key's words, "the broad movements [in the voting] of the electorate appear to be great tides that carry along to some extent all kinds and classes of people regardless of the admonitions of the leaders of even the most disciplined mass pressure groups."[6] His specific evidence on this point is a comparison of trends away from the Democrats after 1936. If unions had enjoyed any substantial capacity to influence union votes in favor of the Democratic Party, it should have been found that union families moved away from the Democrats significantly more slowly than did manual worker families generally. From year to year, however, the movement away was about the same for both groups.

SPECIAL RULES OF THE GAME FOR ACTIVISTS

As an alternative explanation, Key has argued the following: Politics comes to be a kind of a closed game, played by interest-group spokesmen, members of the House and Senate committees, and officials of administrative departments. The game takes something of the "form that it would take if there were no elections or no concern about the nature of public opinion; that is, those immediately concerned make themselves heard in the process of decision." Interest-group leaders will be listened to with respect not because they wield power but because they are perceived to be representatives of interests entitled (by the accepted norms or rules governing the few activists) to be heard and to be accorded consideration. The rules provide that all entitled to play the game should get a fair deal. Having an organization is sometimes necessary to get into the game; beyond that, organizing publicity and other activities of the group are actually only rituals.[7]

Other students of interest groups have given considerable support to such an explanation, although they have not gone as far as Key does in suggesting that the game might take about the same form even if there were no elections. Writing about the influence of interest groups in legislatures, David Truman, for example, concludes that "'pressure,' conceived as bribery or coercion in various forms, is scarcely the distinguishing feature of interest groups in the legislative process."[8] Instead, he says:

It is rather a means of so adjusting conflicting claims upon the government that the underlying expectations about the governing process, some of them written in constitutions and statutes and more of them unwritten, will not be sharply and irretrievably violated. These expectations concerning the "rules of the game" themselves are interests, largely unorganized but overlapping more or less insistently those that appear in more obvious form.[9]

There is, however, still another explanation.

[6] *Ibid.*, p. 522f.
[7] *Ibid.*, p. 526f.
[8] D. B. Truman, *The Governmental Process* (New York: Alfred A. Knopf, 1960), p. 351.
[9] *Ibid.*, pp. 392f.

64

More valid than the previous explanations is this: Interest-group leaders influence the proximate policy maker through persuasion. They try to persuade him that what they want is what he too thinks is best—or that what he should realize is best includes what they want.

Is that all? you may ask. No "pressure"? No tricks? No clever machinations? All these are possible—some officials, for example, are simply bribed. Or seduced by the prospects of a high-paid job on their retirement from government. The big engine of interest-group participation in the play of power, however, is persuasion, and it is powerful indeed.

Persuasion takes many powerful forms, as we have already several times noted in acknowledging irrational and non-rational influences in the play of power. It is often almost without content—more sloganeering. It is often deceitful. It often preys on anxieties not openly acknowledged.

But interest-group persuasion also proceeds through what we have called partisan analysis, all the more when it seeks to reach policy makers whose responsibilities require that they look realistically into the merits of alternative policies and who demand competent analysis because their opponents will be armed with it. Interest groups are highly-skilled practitioners of partisan analysis; and it is perhaps their main source of influence or power. Interest-group leaders help the proximate policy maker to analyze policy implications of his own attitudes and values.

To be sure, an interest group may try analysis of other kinds—even attempting a fundamental alteration of the outlook, political philosophy, most stable principles, or biases of a proximate policy maker. Our hypothesis is, however, that their educational or persuasive work is typically more restricted —specifically, to showing the proximate policy maker how a policy desired by the interest group squares with the policy maker's philosophy, values, or principles. For example:

. . . in 1955 a House committee held a hearing on plans for the Air Force Academy; the architects' preliminary sketches, more or less in the modern style, were of structures using large expanses of glass and quantities of metal after the fashion of Lever House of New York. Frank Lloyd Wright turned up before the committee to dissent from the designs and others criticized the departure from the use of traditional American building materials. Intimations crept in that the plans were a bit radical, even un-American. The Veterans of Foreign Wars took the design as an "insult to our American heritage and traditions." It turned out that the hands behind the scenes guiding the show were those of the Allied Masonry Council and its public relations experts, people interested in the use of brick, stone, and other good traditional American building materials. The council had had in its maneuvers the collaboration of the Hon. John E. Fogarty, Representative from Rhode Island and former president of a local of the Bricklayers Union.[10]

Legislators, executives, and civil servants usually claim that they accede to interest-group requests only when reasonably persuaded; they are not, so they say, coerced, pressured, or hoodwinked. We might dismiss their in-

---

[10] V. O. Key, Jr., *Politics, Parties, and Pressure Groups* (New York: Thomas Y. Crowell Company, 1958), p. 148n.

sistence as evidence of nothing more than their disinclination to admit the humiliation of knuckling under to interest groups. But there is evidence that officials are not on the whole pushed around except by each other and that to be effective interest groups do indeed have to persuade—and with better instruments than misrepresentation.

The most impressive single piece of evidence is a 10-year study, by Bauer, Pool, and Dexter, of foreign-trade policy making.[11] They found that congressmen were heavily dependent on the help of interest groups in analyzing the implications of policies for their own basic values. At an extreme:

> The assistant of [a Congressman] who was a key figure in the reciprocal-trade fight said: "I absolutely had to beat them over the head at our lobbying organization to find out what I wanted to find out; I had to push and push them on this to get the information." And one Congressman, when asked what he had heard from the lobby groups on his side and whether they had pushed him, said: "Hell, no, it's just the other way around; it's me calling them up and trying to shaft them to get off their fat rears and get out and do something." To many a Congressman, the interest organization is a source of information about the attitudes of significant groups in his public, a source of research data and speech material, and an unofficial propaganda ally to help him put his own case forward.[12]

Another excellent study—of state rather than national politics—also stresses the research and advisory role of interest groups, as in a typical comment of a state legislator about lobbyists:

> They can study and present the issues concisely—the average legislator has no time or inclination to do it, and wouldn't understand bills or issues without them. A professional lobbyist in ten minutes can explain what it would take a member two hours to wade through just reading bills. Both sides come around to you, so you can balance off all one-sided presentations (and they're all one-sided).[13]

In short, the proximate policy maker has an underlying set of dispositions. He is faced with policy choices. He has a good deal of freedom or discretion to act as he sees fit. He does not know which policies best match with his basic attitudes or principles. He needs help. Interest groups are important instruments for helping him by showing him with fact and analysis how to reach a decision.

ALLIANCE BUILDING

When a number of interest-group leaders find common interests on which they can join, they increase the probability that they can find a correspondence between the policy they want and the underlying attitudes of the proximate policy makers to whom they must appeal. In the Air Force Academy example, Wright and the masonry industries constituted an alliance.

[11] R. A. Bauer, I. de Sola Pool, and L. A. Dexter, *American Business and Public Policy* (New York: Atherton Press, 1963).
[12] *Ibid.*, pp. 440f.
[13] J. C. Wahlke, H. Eulau, W. Buchanan, and L. C. Ferguson, *The Legislative System* (New York: John Wiley and Sons, Inc., 1962), p. 338.

Interest-Group Leaders

What brought them together was the possibility that they could each get what they wanted, though each for his own reason, by appealing to congressmen's interests in perpetuating American traditions.

If different values appeal to different proximate policy makers, interest-group leaders can cooperate in seeing to it that each proximate policy maker hears of that value to which he is likely to be most responsive. The Employment Act of 1946, a pivotal piece of legislation that formally committed the U. S. government to the task of maintaining full employment and established the President's Council of Economic Advisers, was in some large part the product of such cooperation among a group of unions together with the American Veterans Committee, the NAACP, the National Farmers Union, the National Lawyers Guild, and still others.[14]

A TEST OF THE HYPOTHESIS

If our hypothesis about interest-group power through partisan analysis is correct, it helps explain the extraordinary effectiveness of some interest-group campaigns directed not at legislators or administrators but at the courts. The NAACP, for example, has since 1945 steadily won gains for Negroes in policy on housing, voting rights, transportation, education, and jury duty by bringing case after case into the courts—not simply for the protection of an individual Negro but to induce the court to reconsider judicial doctrine on important questions of policy.[15] Superficially, one might wonder how an interest group could influence the judiciary unless the judges were corrupt. But if interest groups work largely through analysis designed to induce reconsideration of policies by testing their consistency with underlying attitudes and objectives, it is not at all surprising that judges would be drawn toward new directions in policy as inconsistencies between old policies and Constitutional rules are exposed by NAACP cases in the courts.

Bias in Policy Making

In the United States, much of the steam behind the New Left has been generated by its belief that effective political organization is too much a monopoly of the groups that are already favored in society. The poor and the Negro, they say, do not share at all in the power exercised by such organizations as the United States Chamber of Commerce or National Association of Manufacturers, and not very much in that exercised by the AFL-CIO. Even organizations like the NAACP, the New Left will claim, come to be middle-class organizations.

Obviously, interest-group organization is much easier, much better financed, and hence much more effective for the educated and well-off than for the disadvantaged. The use of professional public-relations firms in political persuasion may mean that, more than in an early period, effectiveness in persuasion can simply be bought by those who can afford to pay the bill. A listing of interest groups in the United States will show that they are over-whelmingly business organizations. Among farmers, it is the better-off who

[14] Truman, *The Governmental Process*, p. 363.
[15] C. E. Vose, "Litigation as a Form of Pressure Group Activity," 319 *Annals of the American Acadamy of Political and Social Science* (September, 1958).

Interest-Group Leaders

join farm interest-groups. Generally, frequency of membership in interest groups is strikingly correlated with socio-economic status.[16] Even a League of Women Voters comes to be a league of middle-class, or even upper middle-class, women.

The bias in policy making is of course not limited to interest-group participation. Elected and appointed proximate policy makers are overwhelmingly from the more favored classes; in the federal government 60 per cent of them come from business and professional families. They will therefore seek out and listen to interest-group leaders with whose desires they are already sympathetic. To be sure, officials do not see themselves as representing the interests of some classes against others; rather it is that they see the general interest in the light of their own group affiliations, a phenomenon conspicuous in small-town politics in which, in an easy relation between business and public officials, both see the public interest as equivalent to what they agree on. Every man is, of course, a product of early and continuing indoctrinations reflecting family and group socio-economic status. What is more, the prestige of middle-class attitudes and political preferences is so overwhelming in some countries, the United States included, that many of the disadvantaged themselves subscribe to them, thus endorsing and perpetuating the very bias in policy making against which they might be expected to protest. As a result, it is easy to explain class bias in policy making without reference to any hidden or nefarious activity of interest groups.

Limits on Interest Groups

If, as Key says, interest-group politics is a kind of game in which group demands are accommodated to the extent that they are taken to be legitimate demands, the weight of interest groups in policy making is no greater than the weight given to them by proximate policy makers. That weight is great, of course. If, on the other hand, their powers are largely those of partisan analysis, then, great as they are, they are nevertheless constrained by the fundamental values of proximate policy makers to whom they appeal. Without belittling the great power of interest groups, we take note of certain additional checks:

1. Conflict among interest groups curbs the influence of any one of them.
2. Because many citizens are attached to several organized or unorganized interest groups, their political energies cannot be harnessed exclusively by any one of them.[17]
3. "A disturbance in established relationships and expectations anywhere in the society" may produce out of the unorganized a new interest group to correct the disturbance.[18]
4. Much of an interest group's organizational activity is actually given over to clarifying the implications of policies for its own membership and is therefore not even designed to achieve a direct influence on proximate policy makers.[19]

[16] For a summary of evidence, see Schattschneider, *The Semi-Sovereign People*, pp. 30–36.
[17] Truman, *The Governmental Process*, p. 509.
[18] *Ibid.*, p. 511.
[19] Bauer, *et al.*, p. 398.

Interest-Group Leaders

In the U.S.S.R. there are various groupings of interest in the government and among the millions of persons who participate in the socialized business enterprises of the economy. Some of them, like the trade unions, are formally organized—but not to serve as interest groups. Instead, they are organized to implement government management of the economy. Others of them are not at all formally organized and merely represent clusters of loyalties or factions that are important for determining who rises and who falls in the Soviet system. Sometimes some of these informal groups are eliminated by others. Their leading members, for example, may be removed from seats of power and sent to outlying districts, and the subordinate members thereupon arrange a transfer of their loyalties to the more successful leaders.

In Western-style democracies, interest groups play some such variety of roles as we have identified for the United States. In West Germany, membership in some economic interest groups is required by law, and the groups are used by the government for economic administration. In Britain, although interest groups have very much the same legal status as in the United States, their contact with government is significantly different. In the British Parliamentary system, the authority of Prime Minister and Cabinet, together with party discipline, greatly reduces the authority of the Member of Parliament. Interest-group leaders will therefore spend their time cultivating ministers and members of the Cabinet, party leaders, and high-level administrators. They do, however, also achieve another kind of influence in Parliament: past or present officers of many dozens of business associations are elected to the House of Commons.[21]

In less developed countries, where political participation is at a low level because of illiteracy and poor transportation and communication or because of insufficient experience with mass participation in politics, "the interest articulation" function of interest groups may be (though the case is by no means proved yet) more critical than in the more fully developed democracies. For in these societies, alternatives to interest groups as channels through which the citizen's needs can be called to the attention of proximate policy makers are much less effective than in the developed societies. Journalism, research, and informed public discussion are all thin.

Yet in these very countries interest groups are weak. India, for example, has a structure of interest groups inherited in part from the struggle for freedom. But some of the groups, especially peasant and trade-union groups, are weakened by being subordinated to political parties. Congress Party control over its affiliated trade union, INTUC, for example, sometimes turns INTUC into a propaganda arm of the party at a time when it ought to be warning the Congress of worker disaffection.[22] Many other possible groups are simply not organized.

[20] For a survey, see H. W. Ehrmann (ed.), *Interest Groups on Four Continents* (Pittsburgh: University of Pittsburgh Press, 1958).

[21] S. H. Beer, *British Politics in the Collectivist Age* (New York: Alfred A. Knopf, 1966), p. 376.

[22] M. Weiner in G. A. Almond and J. S. Coleman, *The Politics of Developing Areas* (Princeton: Princeton University Press, 1960).

69

The
Proximate
Policy Makers

C H A P T E R N I N E

If you or I decide to announce that all clocks should be turned ahead
one hour or that a new appropriation should be made for public
housing in our state, nothing would happen as a result
of our announcement. But there are people from whom such an
announcement would in fact set in motion the changes they intended.
They are the proximate policy makers, defined in Chapter Five.

By what act, custom, rule, or procedure does a man play the role
of proximate policy maker? Except in rare circumstances marked by violence,
he does so, we saw, only if authority is conceded to him.

Not all authority is granted by law. During much of Stalin's dictatorship, he was Secretary General of the Party, not a government official. In the United States, some of the old-style bosses held authority in policy making like Stalin's, in that it was authority in a political party yet could be successfully exercised in giving orders to government officials of the highest rank. But most proximate policy makers are government officials.

The titles, tasks, and powers of the principal proximate policy makers of many systems are widely known. To understand just how proximate policy makers play their part in the policy-making process requires that we look further into:

1. certain aspects of the specialized roles of certain kinds of proximate policy makers;
2. how they are organized to cooperate with each other; and
3. how they supplement organized with informal cooperation.

In this chapter we shall look into certain aspects of the specialized roles in the U.S. of President, national and state legislators, and administrators in national, state, and local government.

The President

In his constitutional grants of authority, the President is powerful beyond any other official in American government. He has broader powers of appointment by far than any other official. He oversees the executive branch.[1] He is Commander-in-Chief of the nation's military forces. He is largely responsible for diplomatic negotiations. He can veto legislation. He can do a great deal more, however, than what the Constitution explicitly instructs or permits him to do, and has come to be almost "king and prime minister rolled into one."[2] How does he come to loom so large in policy making? We suggest three answers:

1. *His constitutional authority has been greatly expanded by legal grants of authority by Congress.* As government takes on new functions over the years, some of them, like monetary management, foreign aid, and space exploration, pose technical problems beyond the competence and time that Congress can bring to their solution. When Congress consequently delegates tasks to administrative officials, it further increases the influence of the President on policy simply because of his constitutional authority to supervise the administrators.

In addition, Congress has explicitly loaded onto the President increasing policy-making authority, as in requiring him to recommend to Congress a budget of proposed expenditures for each year. Other acts of Congress illustrate a deliberate expansion, step by step, of presidential policy-making authority: the Railway Labor Act, Taft-Hartley Act, Employment Act, National Security Act, Atomic Energy Act, among others. Each of these instructs the President to take from Congress certain policy-making responsibilities.

[1] Hence, as the federal bureaucracy grows (from a quarter of a million civilian employees in 1901 to 3 million today), the President's tasks and powers grow.
[2] For an extended analysis of the presidency and of the President's relations with

2. *He is granted extra-legal authority because other proximate policy makers at their own initiative offer it to him or because he uses his legal authority to induce them to offer it.* Because leadership in Congress is fragmented through the committee system and because congressmen know that someone or some small group has to take responsibility for organizing a legislative program, congressmen have informally conferred on the President both the authority and the positive responsibility, to the near exclusion of any similar role for themselves, to propose major legislation.[3] Clearly, presidential authority for legislative leadership is now well established.[4]

The President also exercises extra-legal authority as leader of his party. That authority is conceded to him for various reasons. For one, he is the most effective spokesman of his party; what he says commands press coverage to a degree unmatched by the announcements of any other public official. And, again, just as Congress needs leadership, so does the party.

3. *He uses his authority indirectly to intervene in policy matters beyond the direct scope of his authority.* His control over patronage and appropriations, his powers of publicity, the range of favors he can grant, the difficulties he can throw in the way of a legislator's own bills—all rooted in presidential authority—give him indirectly still other powers in policy making. Consequently, he participates at all stages in legislative and administrative policy making. There is no field or phase of policy making into which he cannot reach. Through his broad formal and informal authority, he can always find leverage. President Johnson's announcement in the fall of 1967 of a freeze on certain categories of federal expenditure, well within his authority, was a tactic designed to push congressmen into supporting his proposal for a tax increase. The President had no authority to require congressional assent to his tax increase, but he had at hand a variety of methods of employing his other grants of authority to bring Congress around to his position.[5]

As we move on in later chapters to examine cooperation among proximate policy makers, we shall further clarify the President's role.

Legislators

In fundamentals, the policy-making role of the legislator is familiar. In American government, all policies have to be set by legislative enactment

---

Congress, see N. W. Polsby, *Congress and the Presidency,* Foundations of Modern Political Science Series (Englewood Cliffs, N. J.: Prentice-Hall, Inc., 1964).

[3] R. E. Neustadt, "Presidency and Legislation: Planning the President's Program," 49 *American Political Science Review* (December, 1955), p. 980.

[4] For a history of the conflict over presidential power *vis-à-vis* the Congress, see R. A. Dahl, *Pluralist Democracy in the United States* (Chicago: Rand McNally & Co., 1967), pp. 90ff.

[5] Field by field, the President is aided by the Secretaries of the major Departments of government. Collectively as the Cabinet they do not much assist him, a point worth making because of the contrasting importance of the Cabinet as a collective institution in parliamentary systems. What use the President makes of his Cabinet as a board of advisers depends on the President himself, for the law does not prescribe any collective Cabinet authority. Cabinet members tend to be specialized to their specific tasks and do not develop general competences on policy making on which the President wishes to lean. President Wilson's Secretary of War replied to the Secretary of the Navy's offer of inter-departmental cooperation: "I don't care a damn about the Navy and you don't care a damn about the Army. You run your machine and I'll run mine" (R. F. Fenno, Jr., *The President's Cabinet* [Cambridge: Harvard University Press, 1959], p. 133).

The Proximate Policy Makers

except for policy making delegated to the administrative branches, and the specialized policy making of the courts.

For any elected representative of the people—for President or governor as well as for legislator—an important question is whether he ought to support policies he thinks best, or policies the voters want. For the legislator another question is whether he ought to work for the welfare of all citizens or only of his constituents. The questions are practical ones for the representative himself, and they have long been major issues in political theory.[6]

Legislators in actual fact practice a variety of representative roles. A study of American state legislatures has classified representatives into the following three groups.[7] The *trustee* claims to follow "what he considers right or just." He may not trust people who have axes to grind and who are trying to influence him. He may believe that "if people have the facts, then judgment would be the same as that of the representative." And he may believe that, where he is in disagreement with his constituents, he should try to persuade them. The *delegate* is one who does not use his independent judgment or principled convictions. As one said: "What the district wants me to do is my most important job. . . . If they wanted me to move this capitol, I'd break my neck to do it." The *politico* is one who is a trustee one time and a delegate at another time, or a trustee with respect to some kinds of issues, and a delegate with respect to others.

Which of these roles do most legislators play? In the four states studied, over half the legislators saw themselves as trustees; less than a fifth of them saw themselves merely as delegates; and about a quarter of them saw themselves as politicos.

LEGISLATIVE DISCRETION

The legislator's role is not, however, so simply described. As we have seen, citizens are not well enough informed or sufficiently interested to have opinions on most policy issues. They neither favor nor oppose, say, a treaty to ban proliferation of nuclear weapons. A congressman often cannot therefore be a "delegate" even if he wishes to; he is forced to exercise his own discretion. How does he do so?

In the study of policy making on foreign trade on which we drew heavily in the chapter on interest groups, Bauer, Pool, and Dexter have achieved some major new insights into the policy-making role of the legislator that take fuller account of the discretion enjoyed by legislators. Their analysis runs as follows:[8]

[6] See, for example, Edmund Burke's classic argument that the legislator should be guided by his "enlightened conscience," in his "Speech to the Electors of Bristol" (1774), *Works* (Boston: Little, Brown & Co., 1866), Vol. 2, pp. 89–98. For summary and comment on the historical debate, see C. J. Friedrich, *Constitutional Government and Democracy* (Boston: Ginn, 1946), Ch. 14; and S. H. Beer, *British Politics in the Collectivist Age* (New York: Alfred A. Knopf, 1966), Part I.

[7] J. C. Wahlke, H. Eulau, W. Buchanan, and L. C. Ferguson, *The Legislative System* (New York: John Wiley and Sons, Inc., 1962), pp. 272ff.

[8] The summary of their analysis presented here is largely, though not entirely, in their own words; but for emphasis I have given the analysis a somewhat more formal structure. See R. A. Bauer, I. de Sola Pool, and L. A. Dexter, *American Business and Public Policy* (Englewood Cliffs, N. J.: Prentice-Hall, Inc., 1963), pp. 405 and 478.

73

1. The traditional view of the legislator sees him: (a) as much like a student before a multiple-choice examination, in which he faces fixed alternatives and selects an answer among them, (b) having to choose between following his own best judgment or following the wishes of his constituents.

2. On the contrary, however, the most important part of the legislative decision process is the decision about which decisions to consider.

3. In order to decide which decisions to consider, a congressman must decide what to make of his job, what to do with his time, how to allocate his resources, and where to put his energy.

4. There are so many issues before Congress that every congressman can freely choose to disregard or redefine most of them.

5. He can select those issues which do not raise for him a conflict between his judgment and his constituents' preferences; that is, he can select those issues on which he feels no special tension between his views and those of his constituents.

6. The issues the congressman chooses to deal with are determined by the kind of job he wishes to do: determined thus by his choices about his career, his professional identity, his activities—determined, in short, by the over-all needs of his position rather than by views on any specific policies held by special groups of citizens.

7. Congress is not a passive body, registering already-existent public views forced on its attention by public pressures. Congress, second only to the President, is, rather, the major institution for initiating and creating political issues and projecting them into a national civic debate.

A congressman has a great deal to do other than cope with important policy decisions, and he may decide to make his reputation with the voters other than by the policies he espouses. He may avoid policy making, spending his energies instead, as did Senator Kefauver, on congressional investigations. Or, as many congressmen do, on personal services to constituents and benefits for his locality. Or on becoming a leader in the party electoral machinery. If he makes policy making his conspicuous public business, he still has to choose, for any one session of Congress and perhaps for his political career, the kind of policy issues on which he will be conspicuous. Is it to be foreign policy, agriculture, auto safety, minimum wages, administrative reform, or what? As a senator, John F. Kennedy chose to become active on U. S. policy toward French involvement in Algeria. He made the choice, not his constituents.

LEGISLATOR AND MARGINAL VOTER

Survey Research Center studies have disclosed a discrepancy between a congressman's sense of how much the voters know about where he stands and how much the voter actually knows. The congressman feels that voters know his policy stands better than they in fact do. An important part of the explanation of the discrepancy is that congressmen are sensitive to the margin of voters who take the trouble to make themselves heard on specific issues—for, as we pointed out earlier, marginal swings in the vote make the difference between victory and defeat. What is easy to underestimate, however, is the degree to which the congressman himself can determine, by the policy matters in which he takes an interest, the persons and groups in his constituency that will become active observers of what he does. Hence, even though he feels the pressure of the marginal voter, he does indeed have the kind of discretion that Bauer, Pool, and Dexter find.

74

It was once a common doctrine in political science that administrators, even high-level ones, only administered policies elsewhere determined in the political system—usually in the legislature. We have come to understand, however, that in high enough levels of the administrative system, administrators inevitably *make* policy. Choice of weapons systems by the Department of Defense, of new highway routes by state highway departments, of nuclear testing programs by the Atomic Energy Commission, of level of price support for agricultural commodities by the U. S. Department of Agriculture, all are important policy choices in which administrators play a major proximate policy-making role.

The administrator has to face up to some of the same kinds of choice that a legislator has to face about the direction of his responsibilities. Is he to decide policy issues on the basis of his own best judgment? If so, best judgment about what? The general welfare? The welfare of the clients of his agency? Or is he to disregard his own judgment and try to follow legislative wishes? We can indicate some of the principal patterns that develop.[9]

Tying to Congress or President. An administrator may choose or fall into the position of nearly exclusive responsibility to one or the other of the two major branches of government. The Army Engineers, for example, regard their obligations to Congress as primary, while a competitive organization, the Bureau of Reclamation, sees its responsibilities as primarily to the President.

The tripartite alliance. One common pattern is the development of alliances, each alliance consisting of a bureau or other government agency, the congressional committee that stands in an overseer relation to it, and the interest groups representing its specialized clientele. Such an administrative agency may conceive of its function largely as accommodating the needs of the persons—usually economic groups like farmers, truckers, bankers, wage earners, and so forth—for which the allied interest group speaks.[10]

Interest adjudication. Sometimes the legislative enactment that confers authority on the administrative policy maker remains silent on important controversial policy issues. For an example, in World War II it was necessary to bring employers and unions together for wage stabilization. The two groups agreed to the establishment of a War Labor Board but deadlocked on whether, in exchange for surrendering the right to strike, the union should be permitted to require union membership of all workers in plants with recognized trade unions. President and Congress both dodged the controversy, and an executive order established the War Labor Board without any instructions as to how it should dispose of the controversy on union membership, leaving a compromise to be worked out by the Board itself.[11] Under these circum-

[9] For a fuller discussion, see H. A. Simon, D. W. Smithburg, and V. A. Thompson, *Public Administration* (New York: Alfred A. Knopf, 1959), Chs. 24 and 25.

[10] H. C. Mansfield, "Political Parties, Patronage, and the Federal Government Service," in The American Assembly, *The Federal Government Service: Its Character, Prestige and Problems* (New York: Columbia University Graduate School of Business, 1954), pp. 106–107.

[11] D. Truman, *The Governmental Process* (New York: Alfred A. Knopf, 1960), p. 444.

stances, the administrative policy maker may see no possibility other than to achieve some kind of "fair" compromise of conflicting segmental interests.

Institutional objectives. Some administrative agencies seem to achieve a kind of crystallization of their institutional objectives, the objectives then serving as a relatively adequate criterion for policy making by the agency. How far such an identification of administrators with agency goals can go is illustrated in the following quote.

No experience in Washington during World War II was more amusing or more predictable than that of the businessman who joined the staff of the War Production Board or the Office of Price Administration breathing fire against the "bureaucrats" and their creations. If he stayed for any length of time he often found himself defending the agency or his part of it against critics, resisting demands from outside sources with a vigor he had but lately denounced, and explaining to his friends in the business world that he had not "sold out" and that they did not understand what the agency was up against.[12]

The public interest. Like the legislator who considers himself to be a "trustee," the administrator will sometimes think his overriding obligation is to use his best judgment as to what is in the public interest. Presumably, some of the friction between administrator and congressman in American government is attributable to the administrator's concept of himself as defender of the public interest—as a policy maker able to rise above the congressman's partisanship.

Subordination to party policy. The traditional operating rule for civil servants in the United Kingdom is that they practice strict neutrality. They do not interject their own policy dispositions into policy making but attempt to implement the policy preferences of the political officials above them, who in turn are implementing party policy to which a strong party discipline binds them.[13] Party discipline being weak in the United States, no policy maker can be precisely responsive to party programs; but insofar as the President and principal congressional leaders of his party can agree on a legislative program, there are indeed policy guidelines to which the administrator can subordinate his policy making.

MIXED RESPONSIBILITIES

We have no systematic information about the relative frequency of these alternative patterns of administrative policy making. Clearly administrators do not, if we take their own testimony, claim to be following any one pattern or even any few of these. Here is what an observer says of the mixed responsibilities in decision making of one federal administrative agency. It is a casual, cynical and obviously incomplete statement; but it indicates how difficult it is to describe precisely the policy-making role of the administrator.

About a decade or more ago, we used to ask around Washington, "For whom does the Civil Service Commission work?" We used to reply, "Well, we think it

[12] *Ibid.,* p. 454.

[13] In actual fact, of course, the administrative group in each ministry tends to develop a policy line of its own that to a degree conflicts with the line of the governing party. I. Jennings, *The British Constitution* (Cambridge, England: Cambridge University Press, 1961), p. 138.

The Proximate Policy Makers

works first for its congressional committees, second for the status employees, third for the American Legion in support of veterans' preference laws, fourth for the civil service employees unions, and possibly fifth for the President." Since the end of World War II, the President has moved up in this list but it is difficult to tell just how far.[14]

THE APPOINTMENT PROCESS

The authority to appoint administrators and judges is an important indirect power over policy. Though civil service rules limit the authority to appoint chief executives, high-level policy-making positions fall within executive authority. Governors and presidents (and their counterparts with other systems) systematically try to influence policy by appointing men whose policy tendencies they endorse and by removing those whose policies they dislike. The same play of power that makes policy makes high-level appointments.[15]

DELEGATION FROM ELECTED OFFICIALS TO TECHNICIANS

The delegation of proximate policy making from elected official to appointed official, which is in some respect like the citizen's delegation to elected official, raises questions, of course, about the effectiveness of the elected official's control.[16] We can see the problem in its most acute form in the case of those appointed officials who hold technical skills not understood by those who appoint them.

The technical expert as policy maker is, of course, controlled in various ways. He is appointed and can be removed by elected officials or by the appointees of elected officials. He is constantly scrutinized and challenged by other experts in his field, especially those who represent various interest groups. He is also challenged by his professional colleagues in the universities and research institutions. In the United States, in addition, fragmentation of the tasks of policy making scatters experts throughout the policy-making process, with such overlap of function that they often watchdog each other. President and Congress both have their technicians or experts. So do the many administrative branches. So do the individual congressional committees.

Paradoxically, elected officials owe some of their control over the expert to the fact that he cannot play the classical role of the pure scientist or technician that is sometimes naively prescribed for him. If it were possible to issue to an expert an adequate set of criteria in the light of which he had no other task than to determine scientifically which of several listed policies would best achieve prescribed values, he might be able to work in such isolation from the play of power as to make difficult an appraisal of his competence by other policy makers. To be sure, his professional colleagues could evaluate him; but given the possibility of common biases among professional intellectuals, in any one field, their check alone might be inadequate. Since, however, for reasons given in Chapter Three, no policy analyst can

[14] Reported in M. H. Bernstein, *The Job of the Federal Executive* (Washington: Brookings Institution, 1958), p. 76.

[15] For a detailed account of the complexity of the play of power in appointments, see D. Danelski, *A Supreme Court Justice Is Appointed* (New York: Random House, 1964).

[16] An anxiety converted into a prediction, but unsuccessfully argued, by J. Burnham in *The Managerial Revolution* (New York: The John Day Co., 1941).

play the role of pure scientist, almost all experts remain locked into the play of power, where the values they espouse have to be argued with laymen. On their policy positions in the play of power, non-experts can communicate with them and form judgments that can be brought to bear on their appointment, supervision, and dismissal.

Still, the problem posed by the critical policy-making positions increasingly filled by technicians is not one on which the present structure of the policy-making process gives great ground for confidence. It may be that there lies ahead of us a transformation of policy making as profound as when direct citizen participation gave way to representative government.

Judges

Judges too make policy. In a study of the judicial process, Benjamin Cardozo, later to become Justice of the U. S. Supreme Court, wrote: "The theory of the older writers was that judges did not legislate at all." The view was that the judge interpreted the law but did not make it. "A pre-existing rule was there, imbedded, concealed, in the body of the customary law. All that the judges did was throw off the wrappings and expose the statutes to our view." But the older view is wrong. "Since the days of Bentham and Austin, no one, it is believed, has accepted this theory without deduction or reserve. . . ."[17] When, for example, the U. S. Supreme Court, performing its assigned task of judicial review of legislative acts, laid down, in *Brown v. the Board of Education* (1954), a new rule of law on school desegregation, it clearly did what Congress might have done—that is, make policy. It does so on many issues.

Judge-made law does, of course, extract from history certain guides to policy making that the legislator is not required to employ. Judges are presumably more concerned than are legislators with the principle that the law be uniform and impartial and devoid of prejudice or whim. Judge-made policy is more respectful of precedent than is legislative policy. But where statutes, judicial precedent, and rules of impartiality still leave room for judicial discretion as to what policy should be, how does the judge decide on policy? How does he see his role at a time like this? Some possibilities are:

Prevailing values. On what judges should do—and presumably what he himself did in fact do—when they make policy, Cardozo wrote: "My own notion is that he would be under a duty to conform to the accepted standards of the community, the mores of the times."[18]

The judge's own values. Some judges, however, take just the opposite view, believing that a judge should follow his own judgment of right and wrong rather than community sentiment.[19] In any case, regardless of what a judge believes he ought to do, a judge, like everyone else, is greatly influenced by rearing, group associations, and his particular perceptions.[20]

[17] B. N. Cardozo, *The Nature of the Judicial Process* (New Haven: Yale University Press, 1921), pp. 124ff.

[18] *Ibid.*, p. 108.

[19] F. V. Cahill, Jr., *Judicial Legislation* (New York: Ronald Press, 1952), p. 101.

[20] For a summary statement and bibliography on personal background influences on judicial decisions, see H. Jacob, *Justice in America* (Boston: Little, Brown & Co., 1965), Ch. 1; as well as p. 106 on differences between Democratic and Republican judges.

The Proximate Policy Makers

Balancing of group pressures. Not surprisingly, those political scientists who see politics largely as mutual adjustment among interest groups explain judicial policy making accordingly. Writing about a 1906 Supreme Court case, the "father" of group theories of politics, Arthur S. Bentley, said of the justices: "They are a functioning part of this government, responsive to the group pressures within it, representatives of all sorts of pressures. . . ."[21]

For lack of hard data, we do not know which of these patterns of judicial policy making, or what combination of them, is most common. Presumably, none of these explanations of judicial policy making does justice to the complexity of considerations that enters into a judge's mind.

Much of the literature of jurisprudence strains to cast the judge in the role of a policy analyst who can, at least in principle, find a scientific or rational policy to fit the problem at hand. Justice Oliver Wendell Holmes, for example, wrote: ". . . I have in mind an ultimate dependence upon science because it is finally for science to determine, so far as it can, the relative worth of our different social ends. . . ."[22] In recent years, however, a great deal has been done by political scientists to relate judicial decision making to the play of power. On the basis of a historical comparison of political trends and Court decisions, Glendon Schubert found: "The Court's basic policies remain stable over long periods of time, and changes that do occur reflect very fundamental changes in the general political system, of which the Court is a component part."[23]

In an earlier study of all cases in which the Court has declared federal legislation unconstitutional, Dahl similarly found:

[The Court's] discretion, then, is not unlike that of a powerful committee chairman in Congress who cannot, generally speaking, nullify the basic policies substantially agreed on by the rest of the dominant leadership, but who can, within these limits, often determine important questions of timing, effectiveness, and subordinate policy.[24]

Yet the processes by which judges are induced to take the same path as is taken by "political" leaders needs a good deal more clarification. Empirical studies of actual judicial behavior and the testimony of judges on how they reach decisions on policy are not yet satisfactorily reconciled.

Proximate Policy Makers and Group Interests

A point now worth remarking is that for each type of proximate policy maker, we have found (in this and preceding chapters) a more independent role than some "groupist" theories allow. Let us put what we have said side-by-side with group theories.

[21] A. S. Bentley, *The Process of Government* (1908) (Evanston, Ill.: Principia Press, 1935), p. 393.
[22] Cahill, *Judicial Legislation*, p. 44.
[23] G. Schubert, *Judicial Policy Making* (Glenview, Ill.: Scott, Foresman & Co., 1965), p. 153.
[24] Dahl, *Pluralist Democracy*, p. 168.

The Proximate Policy Makers

Group sources of political opinion? In some group theories of politics, no more is alleged than that political attitude, opinion, orientation, and preference have their origins in group life.[25] Every man is indeed a product of group life. He forms his first appetite and taste in the family group. Through play groups, school groups, and later through play, work, religious, and political groups, and the like, his policy preferences are formed.

This is not to say, however, that the groups that have formed his outlook are interest groups, or even political groups. Nor is it to say that each such group has indoctrinated him with a disposition to do favors for the group. It is from groups that we take both our broadest, most altruistic values—a sense of fair play, compassion, generosity, and some identification with all the peoples of the world instead of our kinsmen alone; and our most narrow values—our concerns for self, family, and locality.

Proximate policy makers as referees of group conflict? One groupist doctrine that goes further is that proximate policy makers are referees of group conflict. Earl Latham has written about legislatures in an oft-quoted statement: "The legislature referees the group struggle. . . ."[26] He goes on to say, "the legislature does not play the inert part of cash register," for proximate policy makers constitute groups themselves. Members of the Senate are a group, so also members of the Senate Committee, or administrators taken as a whole or in sub-groups. So the picture is of proximate policy makers refereeing a game in which they are themselves players. It is their role as referee, however, that is conspicuously played up.

Our view has been that proximate policy makers are much more active in the play of power than as referees. We have seen that *they are the principal players in the play of power,* to whom interest-group leaders, powerful as they are, are subordinated. Even earlier, we saw that one cannot satisfactorily explain politics as a conflict-resolution process.

Policy making as self-serving segmental politics? A corrupted version of the above two views is that almost all interests that enter into policy making serve narrow or segmental group interests. But as we have already seen, the American League to Abolish Capital Punishment is not organized by people who fear they are going to be hanged. There are innumerable groups, we have seen, that pursue not segmental interests but their versions of a public interest. Proximate policy makers, we have seen, pursue their own versions both of segmental or group interests and of widespread or common interests. They do not reconcile conflicts over policy in every case by reference to the interests of some group less than the whole citizenry. They might, for example, go to war to enrich the munitions industry, but they may also go to war because they want the survival of the nation as a common collective value.

[25] D. Truman's *The Governmental Process* goes somewhat further than this view but is nevertheless the fullest statement of it.

[26] E. Latham, *The Group Basis of Politics* (Ithaca: Cornell University Press, 1952), p. 35*f.*

The Proximate Policy Makers

Organized Cooperation Among Proximate Policy Makers

CHAPTER TEN

For the reasons outlined in Chapter Five on the play of power, proximate
policy makers have to cooperate. The rules of the play of power,
especially those concerned with the assignment of authority, require it.
A legislator, for example, can exercise his authority to lay
down policy only in cooperation with other legislators; that is to say,
policy is authoritatively made only by a voted agreement among them.
The Prime Minister of the U. K. can make policy only with the cooperation
of the House of Commons. Rules and authority are so formulated as to both

limit the power of any one proximate policy maker and to achieve the efficiencies of division of labor and specialization.

Because any policy maker can use his authority indirectly to reach into policy areas beyond his own, conflict is pervasive, and the need for cooperation is all the greater.

Central Coordination and Mutual Adjustment

On a naive view, cooperation requires a central coordinating authority. For if men need to cooperate, how better to do it than through a supervisory authority? The fact is, however, that proximate policy makers, like any other men, can arrange cooperation either through central supervision *or* through negotiation, bargaining, and other forms of mutual adjustment.

Which of the two alternatives is more suitable varies from circumstance to circumstance. Some of the same fear of concentrated power that leads men to divide up policy-making tasks often leads them also to refuse to grant supervisory authority to a central coordinator. The American system of checks and balances reflects such a fear. Having set some officials to check and balance others, the men who wrote the Constitution could not consistently then put a central coordinator over the interacting officials.

Fear of concentrated power aside, central coordination is sometimes less desirable than mutual agreement on efficiency grounds. For central coodination may impose analytic and regulatory tasks on a central authority beyond its capacities. Think back on the analysis, in Chapter Three, of limits on man's analytical capacities. *Each limit is also a limit on a central coordinator's capacity to analyze the desired relations among subordinate policy makers and to regulate them.*

All this takes on significance because cooperation is achieved through a mixture of both forms—central coordination and mutual adjustment—in all political systems. We shall see, however, that some systems (the British, for example) rely more heavily on central coordination, and others (the American, for example) more heavily on mutual adjustment.

The tactic of delegation. A common device for arranging cooperation is delegation. A congressman, for example, simply casts his congressional vote according to the instruction of some other proximate policy maker to whom he has delegated responsibility for making the decision. Delegation from many to one or a few achieves a kind of central coordination in the hands of the one or the few who make the decision for the whole group. Delegation from one to one—say, from a congressman to a colleague who he thinks is better informed on an issue—is a case of mutual adjustment.

In the American system, certain restricted forms of central coordination are typically organized somewhat formally; and mutual adjustment is typically arranged informally. Roughly speaking, we shall discuss the organized forms in this chapter and the informal forms in the next chapter. Because, however, some formal devices arrange mutual adjustment and some informal devices are centralized, we cannot make a sharp separation.[1]

[1] For extended analysis of the merits, for rational policy making, of central coordination and mutual adjustment, see C. E. Lindblom, *The Intelligence of Democracy* (New York: The Free Press, 1965).

Organized Cooperation Among Proximate Policy Makers

Achieving cooperation among proximate policy makers is not as simple as might first appear. In American government there are not merely a few proximate policy makers who can engage in easy face-to-face discussion in order to agree on policy. The President—or any one congressman—has to cooperate with more congressmen than he can ever take time to see. Difficulties in achieving cooperation are most clearly seen in the case of the House of Representatives. In an illustrative year, 1963, nearly 10,000 bills and over 1,500 resolutions were introduced in the House, each calling for a decision. Four hundred and thirty-five members cannot handle such a flow without a good deal of organized cooperation. Without it, each member would be called upon to make decisions on matters far beyond his capacities to collect information and exercise independent judgment. His difficulties would be compounded by the speed with which he has to dispose of each policy question, simply because there are so many of them.

Policy making therefore requires organizational machinery even among proximate policy makers; they need a "government within government." And they create such a government within government in various ways—through, for example, the hierarchical organization of administrative policy makers, or through such devices as interdepartmental and interagency committees, of which there are thousands in the U. S. government. One of the major devices for cooperation is the congressional committee system.

The Congressional Committee System

Although in a parliamentary system like that of the U. K. the Cabinet becomes the one committee to which major policy-making responsibility is delegated, in American government there are many legislative committees.[2] In the House are 20 standing committees; and some, especially the Committee on Appropriations, are divided into largely autonomous sub-committees, 13 of them in the case of Appropriations. The most powerful committees are Appropriations, Rules, and Ways and Means. Most of the other committees are organized by subject area: Armed Services, Education and Labor, Agriculture. In the Senate are 15 committees with a proliferation of sub-committees, the division of committee business by subject matter paralleling that of the House. And, again, the committees vary in power and prestige, at least as senators see them. High on the list are Foreign Relations, Appropriations, Finance, and Armed Services.

DELEGATION OF POLICY DECISIONS TO COMMITTEES

The House and the Senate have both largely delegated policy decisions to these committees. With rare exceptions, legislation comes to the floor of the House or Senate only after it has been considered by a committee and carries

[2] Extended analysis and detail on the congressional committee system is in N. W. Polsby, *Congress and the Presidency*, Foundations of Modern Political Science Series (Englewood Cliffs, N. J.: Prentice-Hall, Inc., 1964); The American Assembly, *The Congress and America's Future* (Englewood Cliffs, N. J.: Prentice-Hall, Inc., 1965); and R. K. Huitt, "The Congressional Committee: A Case Study," 48 *American Political Science Review* (June, 1954).

Organized Cooperation Among Proximate Policy Makers

a committee's recommendation. Only a small fraction of the thousands of bills introduced in Congress each year ever survive their committees. In effect, the committees do enough policy making on their own to reduce the explicit policy decisions that must be made by the House or Senate as a whole to a relatively small number. And, of those bills that do emerge from committees, the House and the Senate usually follow the committee recommendations or amend the bills only in minor ways.

Because every congressman belongs to one or more committees, he has an opportunity to be deeply engaged in policy making. But he is typically not a relatively well-informed and active policy maker outside the field of his committee assignments.

The committees can usefully be thought of as a group of independent "little legislatures" bound together by their common obligation to the members of the House and Senate as a whole. They are not tied together in any super committees other than the House and Senate as a whole. Nor do they join together as a coordinating body, steering committee, committee of committees, or legislative cabinet. Each committee—and in many cases, each sub-committee—is to a striking degree autonomous.[3]

When a bill is passed in one form by the Senate and in another form by the House, the chairmen and the most senior members of each of the committees who handled the bill in their respective Houses are appointed to a conference committee to work out an agreed-on form of the bill. The extent of delegation to committees is indicated by the rule in both Houses that the recommendation of the conference committee cannot be amended but must be accepted or rejected in entirety.[4]

DELEGATION TO COMMITTEE CHAIRMEN

If citizens delegate policy-making responsibility to congressmen and congressmen delegate it to committees, so also committees delegate some of it to their chairmen. The rules of the House and Senate concede great authority to committee chairmen. Through appointment of subcommittees and the assignment of bills to the various sub-committees, the chairman can go far to see that a bill will get the kind of committee report that he wants. He also has the power to call or refuse to call committee meetings and hearings; he appoints members of his committee to the conference committee when bills are passed by the House and Senate in different forms; and he has a good deal to say about appointments to his own committee. With his power to block or expedite policy, and with his powers over the advancement in his committee of individual members of the Houses, the committee chairman comes to be a person to whom ordinary members of the House respectfully defer in still other matters. Informally, therefore, his powers over policy making are greater than would appear from his formal authority as committee chairman.[5]

[3] For a vivid and perceptive analysis of how a committee operates, see R. F. Fenno, Jr., "The House Appropriations Committee as a Political System: The Problem of Integration," 56 *American Political Science Review* (June, 1962).

[4] The operation of the conference committee under conditions of strong Senate-House conflict is analyzed in some detail in J. L. Pressman, *House vs. Senate* (New Haven: Yale University Press, 1966).

[5] Polsby, *Congress and the Presidency*, pp. 52ff.; and J. C. Wahlke, H. Eulau, W. Buchanan, and L. C. Ferguson, *The Legislative System* (New York: John Wiley and Sons, Inc., 1962), Ch. 8.

Organized Cooperation Among Proximate Policy Makers

In the fall of 1967 the Chairman of the House Ways and Means Committee announced that he would not accept the President's proposed tax increase until the President presented planned long-term reductions in federal spending. Only a policy maker of great power could so declare himself.

COMMITTEE RESPONSIBILITIES TO CONGRESS AS A WHOLE

Do the committees accurately represent congressional attitudes, and does the position taken by the chairman accurately represent the committee?

The whole committee system, including the large concession of authority to committee chairmen, was created by congressmen themselves. The rules are presumably what the members of each House want them to be. On the other hand, the bare fact is that many bills that would have been passed had they gone to the floor of the Houses have been killed off by their committees. And it is often clear that a large majority will often want to consider a bill that one of its committees refuses to report out for their consideration. How does such a situation come about—that Congress establishes a committee system that produces policies different from those that Congress as a whole would itself endorse if it had the chance?

There are two answers:

1. Because of the limited time a congressman can give to any policy issue and because of the opportunity afforded to the committee system for specialization, a congressman will to a degree trust a committee's judgment even when he is, on the basis of what information he has, in disagreement with it.

2. The congressman wants the committee system to perform several functions for him of which "representing" him is only one, and he is willing to give up some accuracy in the way in which the committee and its chairman represent him in order that the committee and its chairman may more successfully perform the other functions for him.

For example:

Committee assignments are used less to "mirror" the preferences of the House in the committee than to facilitate the reelection of members of the Houses.[6] As an illustration, to help their reelection prospects, representatives of wheat, cotton, and tobacco areas will be assigned to the House Agriculture Committee, where their participation can redound to their credit with the voters back home.

Congressmen will sometimes want to count on a committee to kill a bill that they would be fearful of opposing from the floor. They insulate themselves from responsibility to the citizenry by tying their own hands with a committee system designed to be to a degree beyond control. One such insulating rule is that committee chairmanships shall be awarded according to seniority. The legislators who end up in chairmanships are therefore those who have survived many elections. And who are these? They are the representatives from the safe districts, the districts that year after year vote the same way. Giving a great deal of power to committee chairmen is therefore a way of giving power to those members of Congress least exposed to the voters.

The committee structure of power is attractive to those many representatives and senators who aspire to unusual power in the legislature. Those members of the Houses who are already powerful in policy making because of their committee

[6] N. A. Masters, "Committee Assignments in the House of Representatives," 55 *American Political Science Review* (June, 1961), pp. 345–357.

Organized Cooperation Among Proximate Policy Makers

chairmanships want, of course, to keep their unusual powers. Many others not yet in those positions but wanting an opportunity to rise in power in either House see the committee structure and the powers of the chairman as offering attractive possibilities for advancement.

Executive Leadership in Legislative Policy Making

The same need for organization, delegation, specialization, and leadership that drives congressmen to the creation of a committee system drives them to depend upon "central" executive leadership, especially in the initiation of policies. We already took note, in the preceding chapter, of the degree to which the President has taken over the task of designing a legislative program for each succeeding Congress. Congressmen need a degree of leadership in the coordination of a legislative program that the autonomous committees and their respective chairmen do not provide. These committees themselves, the chairmen themselves, have turned to the President for leadership in policy making.

In American national politics, the following inadequacies of legislative policy making have supported the trend toward executive leadership.[7]

1. *Fragmentation of policy-making responsibility.* If the committee system, as a method for creating leadership and locating responsibility for policy making, is a method of cooperation among legislators, it on some counts aggravates the problem of achieving cooperation. It has not provided for cooperation among committees or among their chairmen. Jealous of their prerogatives, committee chairmen compel central leadership to come largely from the President.

2. *Localism and provincialism.* In an age in which national organizations of businessmen, workers, farmers, and professional people compel government to think nationally, congressmen think locally. They are of course elected to represent an area, not a nation. Moreover, whereas executives and administrative leaders in government, presidents themselves included, tend now to come from metropolitan centers, a majority of congressmen come from small towns and rural areas.

3. *Seniority in committee appointments.* Committee chairmanships go to congressmen who outrank their colleagues in number of years in office. They therefore fall into the hands, as we already noted, of older members from safe districts who are somewhat insulated from voter pressure; they do not go to vigorous leaders.

4. *Congressional overview of administration.* An intermediate result of congressional policy-making incapacity and of the burgeoning of the administrative branch has been growing congressional preoccupation with scrutinizing the work of administrative agencies, especially through budgetary hearings. The result is that congressmen can find their hands full of work even without attending to policy at all.

The result of all these factors? Perhaps 80 per cent of bills enacted into law originate in the executive branch. And the President since World War II has come to determine the legislative agenda of Congress almost as thoroughly

[7] For an excellent discussion, on which this discussion draws, see S. P. Huntington, "Congressional Responses to the Twentieth Century," in The American Assembly, *The Congress and America's Future.*

Organized Cooperation Among Proximate Policy Makers

as the British Cabinet sets the legislative agenda of Parliament. In state government, the same tendency toward executive leadership in policy making is apparent.[8]

Cabinet Government in Britain

How far central coordination through executive leadership can go is best indicated by cabinet government in the United Kingdom. In British cabinet government, proximate policy making has been greatly delegated to one committee rather than to many; and that one committee, the Cabinet, has come to play a combination legislative and executive role different from that played by any one group of proximate policy makers in the United States.[9] Within that committee a great deal of decision making is further delegated to its "chairman," the Prime Minister.

Members of the Cabinet are Members of Parliament who have been selected by the Prime Minister to take responsibility collectively for policy and administration. The Prime Minister and his Cabinet make policy in the specific sense that, except for certain private bills, all legislation presented to Parliament comes from the Cabinet; and, moreover, the Cabinet is required to resign or to dissolve the House and set a date for new elections if its proposals are not accepted by the House of Commons. Though a congressional committee continues regardless of whether party measures are accepted or voted down, the Cabinet continues only as long as its policies are accepted.

With a high degree of party solidarity, members of the party in power in Parliament (whose leader is the Prime Minister and whose secondary leaders are in the Cabinet) will not wish to bring down the Cabinet by an adverse vote. In actual historical fact, no government holding the majority of the seats in Parliament has been defeated in the House of Commons since 1895. In short, Members of Parliament have surrendered to a small legislative-executive body, the Cabinet, and especially to the Prime Minister, most of the immediate policy-making authority that American legislators think essential to keep within their own hands, or at least within the hands of their various committees.

It is noteworthy that a Prime Minister is not merely a presiding officer in the British Cabinet, but a Member of unusual authority. When a Member of the House of Commons is designated as Prime Minister, he chooses his own Cabinet, and he can remove members of it who are not willing to go along with his policies. It is roughly true that he can impose his will on the Cabinet and through the Cabinet on the House of Commons as long as he remains Prime Minister. If he wishes to prevail over his colleagues and insists on it, they have no recourse other than to remove him. A Prime Minister does not, however, use his authority and other power so crudely as this possibility suggests. We will better understand why he does not, how far he can go in imposing policies on his Cabinet colleagues, and how far they can in turn go

[8] D. Lockard, *The Politics of State and Local Government* (New York: The Macmillan Company, 1963), Ch. 12.

[9] I. Jennings, *Cabinet Government* (Cambridge, England: Cambridge University Press, 1959).

Organized Cooperation Among Proximate Policy Makers

in imposing on Parliament, by looking into the coordinating role of the party in policy making.[10]

Cooperation Through Political Parties

As a kind of limiting case, the dominant role that party *can* play in coordinating proximate policy making in a democracy stands out in the British system.[11]

For the Prime Minister and the Cabinet to play their strong policy-making role in the British system, they must enjoy the stable, continuing support of a parliamentary majority. It is necessary therefore that the Prime Minister himself be a member of a continuing majority and that he choose his Cabinet members and other ministers from those who are members of it. It is therefore also necessary that, through party organization, members of a majority in Parliament ally themselves more or less permanently with each other. If they fail to do so, their majority will crumble and their leaders will have to resign or call for a new election.

In the British system the organization of the Members of Parliament into stable party groups is not accomplished only after they have been elected to Parliament, but by means of the electoral process itself. As we saw in an earlier chapter, candidates for Parliament are, with few exceptions, identified closely with one of the major political parties.

It is through the organization of the party within Parliament that parliamentary leaders are chosen and that authority for policy decisions is conceded to them by the other members of the Parliament. At the same time, through party organization within Parliament, members of the majority in the Parliament can join in discussion through which the Prime Minister and Cabinet can be informed about the degree to which their policy proposals are finding or failing to find favor in the ranks of the majority. The need to keep the party united compels Prime Minister and Cabinet alike to listen to ordinary Members of Parliament in their party. For, to repeat, they continue as majority leaders only as long as their party in the Parliament is held together as a majority on each and every important policy issue.

Party leadership is not, however, quite so responsive to rank-and-file sentiment in the parliamentary party as this consultation might imply, for party leadership itself exercises a great deal of control over the selection of candidates to run under the party label. Parliamentary candidates must have the approval of central party leadership, and they will be denied the opportunity to run for reelection under the party label if they do not stay in line with internal party sentiment. The result is that party leaders can be reasonably sure that members of their parliamentary party are going to be in general agreement with what they as leaders wish to do, and will also be disposed to grant them great latitude in policy making.

There is one overwhelmingly important constraint, however, on the

[10] The British system is unique in Western Europe. For other cabinet and parliamentary systems, see G. M. Carter and J. H. Herz, *Government and Politics in the Twentieth Century* (New York: Frederick A. Praeger, 1965), Ch. 3.

[11] R. T. McKenzie, *British Political Parties* (London: Frederick A. Praeger, 1964).

Organized Cooperation Among Proximate Policy Makers

ability of the party leadership to choose just those candidates who will give party leadership a free hand in Parliament. It is, of course, that each party competes for votes with the other major party. Each is compelled to offer a party program, and candidates supporting the program, that can evoke majority support from the electorate.

There will not, therefore, ordinarily be much possibility for significant conflict between party leadership and the rank-and-file member of the parliamentary party. Both loyal to the party platform, they will differ with each other in minor ways, ways that can be accommodated in party discussion. If a fundamental dissatisfaction with party leadership develops, party leadership, though almost impossible to overrule by vote, can be dismissed. Even if the House of Commons majority will not vote out its own Cabinet, the party can change its party leadership—an easier thing to do when the party is out of power than when it is in, but possible in either case. Churchill took over party leadership and the Prime Ministership from Chamberlain at the outset of World War II, the Conservative Party making the change without voting down its own Cabinet.

AMERICAN PARTIES

Party is a weaker device for legislative cooperation in the federal government in the United States and in the governments of most American states. Officials elected on a party ticket will, however, at least loosely bind themselves together in each House of Congress in a caucus, will elect from among themselves such officers as party leader and party whip, and will organize various party committees to arrange for cooperation among party members.[12] Individual legislators can do very little. At least some party grouping is essential to carry a policy successfully through a vote. Conceivably, without a party to bring their views together, the 439 Representatives each could have a different view on each policy issue, and the 30 members of a legislative committee each his own view, too.

Without party structure and leadership in each House there would, of course, be no possibility of generating enough agreement to vote through the President's legislative program—or any other program for that matter. With weak party discipline in the United States, the party achieves only limited cooperation, in any case. On the President's program, for example, party members may or may not support it. The chairman of a congressional committee, for example, may be at odds with the majority leader of his House, although they are of the same party. As everyone knows, Southern Democrats have often cooperated more effectively with Republicans than with Northern Democrats.

Once congressmen or state legislators concede any significant authority to party leaders, the leaders strengthen their hands by extending their authority. They can sometimes hold a legislator to a party program by threatening to deny him a place on the party ticket. "You aren't on the ticket without the support of the party; if you aren't on the ticket you won't get elected."[13]

[12] For extended analysis of party organization in American legislatures, see D. B. Truman, *The Congressional Party* (New York: John Wiley and Sons, Inc., 1959); Wahlke, *et al., The Legislative System,* Ch. 15; and The American Assembly, *The Congress and America's Future,* Chs. 3 and 4.

[13] Wahlke, *et al., The Legislative System,* p. 366.

Organized Cooperation Among Proximate Policy Makers

Another reason for conceding further authority to party leaders is their power to offer a variety of reciprocal favors. "They can do a lot towards seeing whether your bill will get on the calendar and pushing the hearings along." Or: "You get better committee assignments, and you get appointed to interim committees and all kinds of easy assignments like that." And "If you stick with the party, they'll take care of you. Get you a job after defeat."

Legislators, of course, recognize the need to have a publicly identified program if they are to take advantage of the help of the party and of a party label at election time. "There has to have been some force to hold the majority together, so that you can go home and say, 'this is our program.'" Still another reason for following party leadership is every legislator's admitted need—sometimes desperate need—for information and advice. As we have already seen, no congressman can be well informed or well prepared on any but a small number of issues. "If you are in doubt, right or wrong, follow the party—and there's always something that's in doubt."[14]

The party system interacts with the committee system. Of the most senior members of any legislative committee in the Congress, it is the most senior member of the party having the majority who wins the chairmanship. The assignment of newly elected members of Congress to committees is delegated to party leadership, and the rule is followed that the party in power should have a majority on each committee roughly proportional to the size of its majority in the House as a whole. In short, it is through party organization that the majority in Congress as a whole achieves such control as it enjoys in each of the "little legislatures" that carry on the policy-making work of Congress.

AUTHORITARIAN PARTY SYSTEMS

Parties can do more to achieve cooperation among proximate policy makers than helping to organize the legislative process, and we can see more clearly their other contributions by looking at their role in systems in which the legislative process is absent or, as in the Soviet Union, is a dummy. The Communist Party in the Soviet Union has several functions. It is an apparatus for vast propaganda. It is also a device for policing public administration in general, the administration of economic enterprises, and the military. We want to ask about its role in proximate policy making.[15]

The Soviet system needs cooperation among its proximate policy makers for some of the same reasons as in the case of democracy. There will have to be in the Soviet system, as well as in our own, a division of labor and a specialization among policy makers. There will therefore have to be some kind of integration or coordination of these specialists. Inevitably there will also be, as in the democracies, overlapping authority that will require cooperative adjustment, even though a one-party authoritarian state will not practice the deliberate fragmentation of authority that is practiced in the democracies.

[14] For strategies of party leaders to induce legislative cooperation, see J. D. Barber, "Leadership Strategies for Legislature Party Cohesion," 28 *Journal of Politics* (May, 1966).

[15] On the intertwining of government, party, and factions in Soviet policy making, see F. C. Barghoorn, *Politics in the U. S. S. R.* (Boston: Little, Brown & Co., 1966), Ch. 7.

Organized Cooperation Among Proximate Policy Makers

Moreover, some authoritarian regimes are committed to the "total" reconstruction of society, and hence to a coordinated and thoroughgoing impact on every aspect of society—family organization, child training, religious belief, attitude towards society and the state, individual responsibility, economic organization, and so on. In the thoroughness and comprehensiveness with which public policy intervenes in every aspect of life, such a regime requires great feats of coordination of policy not required in democratic regimes, which entertain more modest policy objectives.

But why a party? With an authoritarian ruler at the top, why cannot the institutions and offices of government itself be used to achieve the cooperation of all policy makers below the ruler? One answer is that even a ruler would want, for purposes of establishing his leadership in policy making, a smaller organization with membership more carefully selected, and with loyalties more manipulable than the organization of government as a whole. Just as he would need such an organization to capture control of the government, so also would he need it to perpetuate his control. He would need an organization that is not merely obedient to the head of state, but to him personally as the only acceptable head of state.

In short, no man alone can control a government. It takes an organization to control a government. And no one man or small group of men can do all the policy making for a government. It takes an organization to organize a sufficient number of policy makers.[16]

If a Khrushchev wants, as he did, to inaugurate a new policy for agriculture, he will use not the formal governmental machinery but the party machinery to begin a discussion of his proposals, for only in the latter are the discussants sufficiently disciplined to participate in genuine debate without overstepping the bounds of their commitments to the over-all program of the Communist Party and their loyalties to their Khrushchev. And only because of the bonds of party can he be confident that policy makers in various fields, within and outside of agriculture, will adjust their own policy decisions to the innovation he desires. He cannot give detailed orders to all policy makers; he cannot review all of them. A cadre of party members operating under party discipline and placed at strategic points for proximate policy making will serve his purposes.

[16] But if a party organization is required in order to control a government, is still another organization required to control the party? Indeed it so appears; and there will therefore be factions, even in the Communist Party of the Soviet Union, with the top leadership in the dominant faction. And there may be factions within factions.

Organized Cooperation Among Proximate Policy Makers

Informal
Cooperation
Among
Proximate
Policy Makers

To a romantic or conspiratorial mind, politics
is wheeling and dealing, organizing "behind the scenes,"
and cleverly outmaneuvering an adversary.
Policy is made in the intimacy of a smoke-filled
room. The more formal processes of government
are deprecated as façade.

  It is just this kind of wheeling and dealing, just this kind
of manipulation, and just this kind of informal interplay
that we are going to discuss in this chapter.

We see such processes of informal interplay, however, in perspective. They are only a part of "politics," only a part of the policy-making process. They are an important supplement to the more formally organized methods for arranging necessary cooperation among proximate policy makers. And we want not a gossipy account of them but a stark identification of their distinctive characteristics.

Mutual Adjustment

The most common method of bringing proximate policy makers into agreement with each other is their own informal efforts toward mutual adjustment. Hierarchical organization, committee systems, executive leadership, cabinets, and party organization are islands of formal organization in a sea of informal mutual adjustment. Proximate policy makers are always signalling, persuading, influencing each other in innumerable informal ways in order to achieve cooperation among themselves—or, as any one proximate policy maker sees it, in order to get others to go along with him.

Mutual adjustment has to do more than arrange such necessary cooperation as formal methods fail to achieve. It must also cope with problems of cooperation spawned by the formal methods. In the U. S., the congressional committee system, developed to organize congressmen cooperatively into subgroups, has created new difficulties of cooperation at a higher level because of the relative autonomy of each committee and of its chairman. In August, 1957, the Chairman of the House Rules Committee, wanting to kill a civil rights bill, simply left Washington for his home in Virginia, leaving his committee without the power to call itself to order to act on the bill. It was not an uncommon tactic.[1] Lacking adequate formal devices of central coordination of committee chairmen, Congress counts heavily on their entering into informal arrangements with each other.

As in the case of the committee chairmen, every concession of authority to a "central" coordinator gives rise to at least some new problems in coordinating the coordinators. The problem is exacerbated because of the freedom already noted with which any proximate policy maker can use his authority indirectly to intervene in policy making in areas outside his authority, as when Congress forbids administrative appointments that lie within the President's authority by withholding legislation until he yields on appointments. The more grants of coordinating authority to selected officials like committee chairmen or party leaders, the more the opportunities for employing authority indirectly. If proximate policy makers can in this way reach into each other's area of authority, sometimes in unpredictable ways, inevitably *ad hoc* informal negotiations or similar arrangements will be required.

RULES GOVERNING MUTUAL ADJUSTMENT

In their informal cooperative arrangement, proximate policy makers, like everyone else in society, are regulated by the universal rules of behavior that constrain coercion and deceit, and impose obligations. But tied together in close interchange by their obligations to make policy, they develop appropriate

[1] N. W. Polsby, *Congress and the Presidency*, Foundations of Modern Political Science Series (Englewood Cliffs, N. J.: Prentice-Hall, Inc., 1964), p. 73.

Informal Cooperation Among Proximate Policy Makers

specific forms of these universal rules, as well as other specialized rules governing their play of power.

One powerful and easily overlooked universal rule in social interchange generally is the rule of reciprocity. Its particular application varies from society to society and from group to group, but everywhere it imposes some obligation on every individual to return favor for favor. In a study of the rule of reciprocity, the sociologist Alvin Gouldner has suggested that the rule is perhaps as universal an element of culture as is the incest taboo.[2] In the House and Senate "reciprocity is a way of life." The rule imposes obligations to trade votes and to exchange other favors as well. An administrative assistant to a senator says: "My boss will—if it doesn't mean anything to him—do a favor for any other Senator. It doesn't matter *who* he is. It's not a matter of friendship, it's just a matter of I won't be an S.O.B., if you won't be one."[3]

There are many other rules, however. Asked what rules of the game they perceive in their own legislatures, legislators in four states reported dozens, of which the following are a sample:

Respect for other members' legislative rights: Support another member's local bill if it doesn't affect you or your district; don't railroad bills through; don't appear before another committee (than your own) to oppose another member's bill; don't steal another member's bill; respect the rights of a bill's author; accept author's amendments to a bill.

Advance notice of changed stand: Notify in advance if you are going to change your stand or can't keep a commitment.

Openness in opposition: Don't conceal your opposition; notify in advance if you're going to oppose or introduce amendments.

Conciliation: Be willing to compromise; don't be a perfectionist; accept half a loaf.[4]

Rules governing behavior are of course violated in varying degrees. But legislative bodies have methods for enforcing their informal rules. The rule breaker will find his own bills held in check, or he may be ostracized from consultations among his colleagues, or he may find opportunities for advancement in the legislature obstructed. Favorable assignments go to what representatives call a "responsible" member of the House. He is one who has a "basic and fundamental respect for the legislative process and understands and appreciates its formal and informal rules."[5]

Methods of Adjustment

What are the specific forms of informal mutual influence in the play of power among proximate policy makers?

[2] A. W. Gouldner, "The Norm of Reciprocity: A Preliminary Statement," 25 *American Sociological Review* (April, 1961), p. 171.

[3] D. R. Matthews, *U. S. Senators and their World* (Chapel Hill: University of North Carolina Press, 1960) (in which the rule of reciprocity in the Senate is further analyzed), as quoted in J. D. Barber (ed.), *Political Leadership in American Government* (Boston: Little, Brown & Co., 1964), p. 175.

[4] J. C. Wahlke, H. Eulau, W. Buchanan, and L. C. Ferguson, *The Legislative System* (New York: John Wiley and Sons, Inc., 1962), pp. 146–147.

[5] N. A. Masters, "Committee Assignments in the House of Representatives," 55 *American Political Science Review* (June, 1961), p. 352.

94

The common answer is "bargaining." Many political scientists see bargaining as a fundamental political process. Some have come close to asserting that bargaining is the central political process and that skill in bargaining is the definitive skill of the politician. For example:

> For the politician is, above all, the man whose career depends upon successful negotiation of bargains. To win office he must negotiate electoral alliances. . . . Most of his time is consumed in bargaining. This is the skill he cultivates. . . .[6]

Others have gone so far as to say that for resolving conflict—and presumably, therefore, for making policy—there are only two possible methods: analytic and bargaining.[7]

But "bargaining" turns out to be an imprecise answer to our question. If, as in the second view, "bargaining" is the only alternative to analytic policy making, then "bargaining" so defined must be roughly synonymous with the term "the play of power," for we have divided the possibilities for policy making into analytic policy making and the play of power. If so, "bargaining" so defined is a catch-all for a variety of methods of policy making; it will not help us much in the specific analysis of informal cooperation through mutual adjustment.

We shall therefore proceed to sort out techniques of mutual adjustment. We will find that there are more of them than are ordinarily embraced in the concept of bargaining, and we shall also find distinctive differences among the techniques that are indiscriminately embraced in "bargaining."[8]

NEGOTIATION

One of the most commonplace forms of mutual adjustment—one of those called "bargaining"—occurs when two or more policy makers enter into explicit negotiations with each other in order to try to reach an explicit basis for cooperation. But negotiation itself takes several forms.

Mutual persuasion. Sometimes the negotiators do no more to influence each other than point out for each other that the facts are different from what they have been thought to be, or that a policy that one negotiator believes he wants does not actually serve his own interests. This is negotiation through the persuasion of partisan analysis.[9] In this kind of interchange (which, we have repeatedly stressed, is powerful indeed), neither policy maker threatens the other or promises any benefits to the other except those that emerge from re-analysis of the problem at hand. Even a powerful president relies on it: in his *Presidential Power*, Richard E. Neustadt writes: "The essence of a Presi-

---

[6] R. A. Dahl and C. E. Lindblom, *Politics, Economics, and Welfare* (New York: Harper and Row, 1953), p. 333.

[7] J. G. March and H. A. Simon, *Organizations* (New York: John Wiley and Sons, Inc., 1958), p. 130.

[8] The fuller array of techniques on which this discussion is based is in C. E. Lindblom, *The Intelligence of Democracy* (New York: The Free Press, 1965), Chs. 3, 4, and 5.

[9] In any specific interchange between policy makers A and B, A may persuade and B may listen, though ordinarily if B listens he also tries to persuade. The other devices of informal mutual adjustment can also be either unilateral or bilateral.

Informal Cooperation Among Proximate Policy Makers

dent's persuasive task with congressmen and everybody else, *is to induce them to believe that what he wants of them is what their own appraisal of their own responsibilities requires them to do in their interest, not his.*"[10]

Exchange of threats and promises. Some people mean by bargaining to refer to the situation of "Unless you do this, I'll . . ." and "If you do that for me, I'll do this for you. . . ." The rules of the democratic game do not permit highly coercive threats of deprivation such as are effective among, say, leaders of the Soviet Communist Party. But a committee chairman can, for example, sometimes have his way with the Majority Floor Leader because he can use his authority to threaten not to report a bill out to the floor of the House unless he gets a concession that he asks for from the Floor Leader. A mutual exchange of promises of benefit is commonplace. Senator Douglas has described the way in which, for example, a public-works appropriation bill is passed:

. . . This bill is built up out of a whole system of mutual accommodations in which the favors are widely distributed, with the implicit promise that no one will kick over the applecart; that if Senators do not object to the bill as a whole, they will "get theirs."[11]

CREATING AND DISCHARGING OBLIGATIONS

Aside from forms of negotiation, policy makers erect upon the rule of reciprocity a vast superstructure or network of mutual obligations that can be created and discharged by the exercise of their respective authority. Sometimes an obligation is created, or one called in, in explicit negotiation, but the exploitation of reciprocity for cooperation in policy making does not necessarily require negotiation.

If, for example, in the Democratic Party the Northern liberals voluntarily concede a point on racial policy to Southerners when the party platform is written in convention, it can count on some concession from the Southerners in return. The understanding may be tacit. The obligation created by the concession is not necessarily part of a bargain, for at the time the concession is made by the Northerners, they may have no demand in mind, preferring merely to count the obligation thus created as "money in the bank" on which they can draw at any time in the future. If, in interdepartmental negotiation, an administrative policy maker from the Department of Defense concedes something to a representative of the U. S. Treasury, he can often expect a reciprocal concession at some later date. He has struck no bargain, but he has stored up a stock of goodwill on which he can later draw.

Much of Lyndon Johnson's influence on policy making when he was Senate Majority Leader can be traced to his diligent investment in laying up a stock of obligations owed him, creating a network around himself. Obligations induce cooperation in such a network not only because any one policy maker who wants to influence a second policy maker can count on the discharge of the obligation the second owes to him. It is powerful also because every proximate policy maker, wishing to lay up a fund of obligations in his favor, is disposed to accommodate himself to other policy makers as a general rule, and as broadly and as frequently as he can, at that.

[10] (New York: John Wiley and Sons, Inc., 1960), p. 46.
[11] Barber (ed.), *Political Leadership in American Government,* p. 175.

Informal Cooperation Among Proximate Policy Makers

Every policy maker operates in an immediate environment that offers him certain opportunities and deprives him of others. One way a policy maker can influence a second policy maker is to try to use his authority to manipulate directly the environment—specifically, the immediate circumstances—in which the second policy maker acts.[12]

In the 1950 struggle between the United States Treasury and the Federal Reserve Board over the short-term rate of interest, the Treasury hit on a strategy to head off the Board's attempts to increase the rate. It made advance announcements of the low-interest terms on which it would sell new bonds, leaving the Board in the position of either going along with Treasury terms or facing presidential and congressional criticism, as well as weathering disturbances to monetary policy if the Board failed to support the market for United States bonds on the Treasury's terms.

For another example, in 1957 Senator Neuburger and other conservationists had proposed that the federal government buy up shares of the dissolving Klamath Indian reservation to keep the land out of the hands of logging companies. Before Senator Neuburger presented a bill to the Senate, however, Secretary of the Interior Seaton proposed a bill that, by giving Senator Neuburger something of what he wanted, drastically altered the possibilities that Neuburger could get all of what he wanted. Seaton's bill would have permitted sales to the logging companies of shares of the reservation, but allowed cutting only under strict government supervision. Senator Neuburger described the effect of this move on him:

> Now the dilemma was mine. If I insisted on my own bill and it bogged down in a partisan political debacle, the economy of my native state would suffer grievously. I desperately needed the unified backing of all my colleagues on the Indian Affairs Subcommittee if we were to have any chance of success with the Senate as a whole. And if only one or two large blocks of Indian timber were purchased privately under the Interior Department's bill, its total cost would be $90 million as contrasted with $120 million under my original bill. This was decisive with me, for I knew that many of my fellow Western Senators—rebuffed on relatively small reclamation and public-works projects in their own states— would wonder why scores of millions of dollars were necessary to buy an Indian reservation in Oregon.
>
> I took the bill which Secretary Seaton had sent to me and dropped it in the Senate hopper "by request." If I had not crossed the Rubicon, I at least had crossed the Upper Klamath Lake. It was my bill now.[13]

Mutual adjustment is all the more complex because each of the above methods for mutual adjustment can be practiced indirectly through third persons. If a committee chairman cannot influence another committee chairman by any of these techniques, he may be able to use these techniques to

[12] Notice that all the techniques of mutual influence rest overwhelmingly on either persuasion or authority.

[13] A. M. Scott and E. Wallace (eds.), *Politics, U.S.A.* (New York: The Macmillan Company, 1961), p. 36.

Informal Cooperation Among Proximate Policy Makers

influence still some other congressional leader, who in turn can get at the committee chairman.

A pressing problem, for example, to the incoming administration of President Kennedy was to induce the House Committee on Rules to permit consideration of liberal legislation on the floor of the House. The President's principal direct move was not directed at the committee at all but at the Speaker of the House to induce him to approach the Rules Committee. The Speaker then negotiated with the Chairman of the Rules Committee to win him over to an expanded committee with increased representation of liberals. This failing, he subsequently tried to replace one conservative member of the committee with a more liberal member, but was dissuaded by protests. He then undertook—indirection again—to induce the membership of the House to enlarge the committee over the objections of its chairman.[14]

ADAPTIVE ADJUSTMENTS

Finally, an obvious possibility is that a policy maker achieves cooperation not by trying to manipulate others but by adapting himself to them—at an extreme by delegating to them. Every overburdened congressman is likely to seek, for each of the unfamiliar issue areas in which he has to act, a fellow congressman to whose specialized competence he will defer in policy making. On his field of competence, some others may defer to him.[15]

A conspicuous area of mutual deference is among subcommittees of the House Appropriations Committee.

Conflict among subcommittees (or between one subcommittee and the rest of the Committee) is minimized by the deference traditionally accorded to the recommendation of the subcommittee which has specialized in the area, has worked hard, and has "the facts." . . . "It's a matter of you respect my work and I'll respect yours."[16]

Deferential adaptation of one's own policy to those of other policy makers may be only partial; that is, a policy maker may calculate just how much he has to yield in order to reach agreement with other policy makers. Toward the end of World War II, President Roosevelt debated whether to determine reconversion policy by executive order, as he was empowered to, or by acts of Congress. At that time Roosevelt apparently believed executive orders to be superior to new legislation for guiding reconversion back to a peacetime economy; but, fearful of Congressional reaction to heavy reliance on executive orders, he made a calculated adaptation to the Congress by asking it for legislation to convert the Office of War Mobilization into the Office of War Mobilization and Reconversion, and by cooperating with it on other reconversion legislation.

[14] A. F. Westin (ed.), *The Uses of Power* (New York: Harcourt, Brace and World, Inc., 1962), pp. 15ff.

[15] R. A. Bauer, I. de Sola Pool, and L. A. Dexter, *American Business and Public Policy* (New York: Atherton Press, 1963), p. 437.

[16] R. F. Fenno, Jr., "The House Appropriations Committee as a Political System: The Problem of Integration," 56 *American Political Science Review* (June, 1962), pp. 310–324.

Informal Cooperation Among Proximate Policy Makers

These informal methods of arranging cooperation intertwine with the more formally organized methods described in the preceding chapter. In particular, party leadership strives to facilitate informal mutual adjustment, primarily among party members but sometimes between the parties. A critically important policy-making specialist, therefore, is the broker, the arranger, the peacemaker. As Senate Majority Leader, from 1953 to 1960, Lyndon Johnson was extraordinarily effective in the brokerage function. He made it his business to know what each senator wanted and how much he wanted it. It was then possible for him to bring a group of senators together for bargains and alliances. Left to themselves, they would not always have recognized their common interests. In an extreme, a broker is not much interested in whether this or that policy wins; he is concerned only that some policy emerges, that the political work of policy making gets done. As majority leader, Johnson approached this extreme and consequently "could arrange for solutions and compromises which would have been unimaginable to an equally constructive but a more committed man."[17]

Mutual Adjustment in Authoritarian Regimes

These same techniques of mutual adjustment—played, however, by rules that permit deceit and coercion to a degree unacceptable in democratic societies—are essential to policy making in authoritarian systems. During the Second World War, for example, German policy toward Russia was subject to a constant tug-of-war among several groups, one including Himmler, Bormann, and Hitler himself, another around Alfred Rosenberg, a third around Goebbels, and a fourth of professional soldiers and diplomats.[18] There were no specialized structures, such as those discussed in the preceding chapter, sufficient to bring these groups together on policy; and whatever cooperation they were able to achieve is largely to be explained in terms of such mechanisms as we have just outlined.

At the highest levels of policy making in authoritarian systems, methods for mutual adjustment are critical because top policy makers are small in number and are therefore thrown into face-to-face communication. In the Soviet Union the Presidium of the Communist Party has only about a dozen members, and sometimes policy is discussed only by an inner circle of the Presidium. The decision to withdraw the missiles from Cuba was, for example, apparently made by informal consultation between Khrushchev and Mikoyan, Brezhnev, Kozlov, Suslov, and Kosygin.

That powerful men can come so peacefully to an informal agreement on policy is not so surprising as might at first seem. In the first place, they are all loyal to an overriding ideology, as is not the case in democratic regimes. Secondly, continuing important differences in policy views among them lead to the ouster of one group by another until the surviving group is relatively homogeneous in its political views. Thus the harsher techniques of mutual adjustment, to which we referred above, will not be brought to bear directly

[17] Polsby, *Congress and the Presidency*, p. 45.
[18] G. Fischer, "Der Fall Wlassow," *Der Monat* (June, 1951), pp. 263*ff.*

Informal Cooperation Among Proximate Policy Makers

on reconciling differences on policy, but indirectly in recruiting into or rejecting from the top policy-making group.[19]

Permutations and Combinations

Endless variety is possible in the pattern of influences brought to bear on a policy through informal mutual adjustment. Each policy-making situation is likely to differ in some important respect from every other. We can never fully understand how any specific policy outcome is achieved without taking account, therefore, of some unique elements in the pattern of mutual adjustment through which the policy is decided on. But because at least those elements are unique, even if we see an understandable recurrent pattern in most of the forces impinging on the policy, we cannot be sure just what the weight of the unique elements is, or the specific character of their influence on the outcome. We can never therefore wholly explain why a particular policy is what it is.

Skill in mutual adjustment—in making the most of one's power in informal interaction—is a distinctive "political" skill. Some proximate policy makers and other leaders are more skilled than others. And some leaders learn how to win what they want in some kinds of situations, but not in others, one leader being skilled in negotiation, for example, and another in direct manipulation. The influences that will successfully be brought to bear on any given policy outcome typically include, therefore, a combination of skills with some significant unique elements. Again, consequently, we can never wholly explain just why this or that policy was arrived at—or will be arrived at.

Nor shall we achieve as sure a competence as we might wish in re-designing the policy-making system when from time to time we see remediable faults in it. For man's design of the system never controls specifically and precisely—but only within broad limits—how proximate policy makers will practice the arts of mutual adjustment. Moreover, as we have repeatedly noted, every new grant of legal or extra-legal authority opens up new possibilities for exploiting that authority indirectly in various techniques of mutual adjustment. The consequence is that reform or redesign of the rules of the policy-making system, especially redesign of the organized forms of cooperation among proximate policy makers, inevitably throws new informal, indirect powers into the hands of various policy makers in unpredictable ways.

[19] For more details see Z. Brzezinski and S. P. Huntington, *Political Power: USA/USSR* (New York: Viking Press, Inc., 1964), pp. 193–224.

Informal Cooperation Among Proximate Policy Makers

Reconstructing Preferences

CHAPTER TWELVE

Now, finally, after tracking down the principal characters
in the play of power, examining their methods of interaction,
noting the discipline of the rules under which they interact, and finding
much of their respective powers to be located in authority and in the
persuasiveness of policy analysis, we can now turn to look at the
policy-making process as a whole.

   In an overview, a first point to be made, and *the* point
of this chapter, is that the policy-making system is not in any regime
merely a process that turns out policies. For any policy-making

system has a prodigious effect on the very preferences, opinions, and attitudes to which it itself also responds. It is not, therefore, a kind of machine into which are fed the exogenous wishes, preferences, or needs of those for whom the machine is designed and out of which come policy decisions to meet these wishes, preferences, or needs.[1] The machine actually manufactures both policies *and* preferences.

How the System Molds Demands on Itself

As now should be apparent, political preferences are pliable, not fixed. In the first place, there are no fixed bed-rock political preferences or wishes. To be sure, men must eat; but what they should eat, how they should eat, and whether some should eat better than others are matters on which opinions vary. Secondly, even if man has to eat to live, the political system may not respond to his need for food. It can let him die, and most political systems do let some of their citizens die. In short, a biological need or other allegedly fixed need may or may not become a relevant political preference, depending on the response of participants in the policy-making process.

Thirdly, what we ordinarily call political preferences—whether of citizens in a democracy or of authoritarian rulers—are not themselves stable objects of subjective desire or preference (like food, warmth, or affection). Rather, they are policies or effects that appear to be useful for achieving such subjective goals (like Medicare or economic growth). As circumstances change, or as the facts come in, our one-time intermediate preferences are amended or abandoned in favor of others. We ask for a change in policy in Vietnam not because our subjective preferences have changed but because we take a new view of the consistency of policy with our subjective preferences. Every new fact or experience remolds our policy preferences.

If for these reasons political demands or preferences are pliable, it is easy to see—and we have seen—that the policy-making process itself molds them. It is in large part from their participation in the system that participants learn how to formulate policy positions, what positions are feasible, and how to tailor a position to increase the chances of success with it. Participants in policy making will, for example, take a position on a policy only after appraising its possible effects. How do they appraise? Partly by looking at the system's past failures and successes with similar policies; partly through the partisan analyses through which all of the most active participants constantly alter the preferences of each other. For another example, when new demands are selected for the crowded agenda of the political system, they do not simply come into the system from outside but are instead decided upon by interest-group leaders, party officials, and official proximate policy makers.[2] We have also seen that citizens take their positions in large part *from* political parties.

Clearly, insofar as every participant has to adjust his position to those of others in order to find support, his politically relevant positive demands are in large part a product of the policy-making system itself. For he must take

[1] As in D. Easton, *A Framework for Political Analysis* (Englewood Cliffs, N. J.: Prentice-Hall, Inc., 1965).

[2] We cannot even identify our self-interest independently of our roles in the political system. R. A. Bauer, I. de Sola Pool, and L. A. Dexter, *American Business and Public Policy* (New York: Atherton Press, 1963), pp. 127*ff.*, 472*ff.*

Reconstructing Preferences

positions suited to the dominant sentiments and states of readiness of the on-going system in which he participates. He begins to push for a minimum guaranteed income, for example, only when the policy-making system comes to a point at which there is some possibility of achieving it.

How a Democratic System Simultaneously Molds and Responds

We need to see, therefore, the democratic policy-making process as both responding to and forming preferences and opinions. For the United States, we can imagine a policy-making ladder with the President at the top and the apathetic non-voting citizen at the bottom. In between are all the other participants, in some such order as the following.

THE POLICY-MAKING LADDER

President

Congressional and other Top Party Leaders, Congressional Committee Chairmen, Top Administrators, and Supreme Court Justices

Other Legislative Leaders, Policy-Making Judges, and High-Level Administrators

Ordinary Legislators and Some Administrators

Lower-Level Party Leaders, Interest-Group Leaders, and Major Public-Opinion Leaders

Politically Active Citizens

Ordinary Voters

Non-Voters

Drawing on the evidence of all the preceding chapters, we know that influences moving up this ladder constrain, instruct, command, permit, and otherwise bend the higher-level participants to the wishes of those at the level below them. At the same time, influences moving down this ladder shape the positions taken at each lower level.

Seen in the large as a two-way communications process, what moves up the ladder is communication on what is wanted; what moves down the ladder is communication on what is possible or most feasible, although both misinformation and non-rational appeals are also sent down. What is wanted is endlessly reconsidered in the light of what is possible or most feasible. What is possible and feasible is constantly reconsidered—and the possibilities themselves reconstructed—in the light of what is wanted.

A number of specific features of the ladder should be noted:

1. At every step of the ladder, at least some more active, informed, or responsible participants in policy making pass information on what is possible, **103**

feasible, and, in their opinion, desirable, downward to less active, less informed, or less responsible participants. In earlier chapters we found this relation between the informed and the uninformed citizen, between candidate and voter, between party leader and candidate, and between President and congressman, among others.

2. At every level, the participant who wants information and advice can choose among competing (and mutually criticizing) sources of information (and misinformation) and advice. In earlier chapters, we saw citizens do so in choosing among interest groups, uninformed citizens do so in choosing among their more informed associates, and congressmen do so in choosing among congressional leaders.

3. Because many of the sources of information and advice (interest-group leaders and competing candidates for office, for example) compete for followings, they are highly motivated to out-perform their rivals in offering pertinent information and advice to those looking for it, although they compete in other less rational ways as well. We have seen, for example, that a union leader, newspaper editor, congressman, priest or minister, and politically active acquaintance all compete for the citizen's attention by offering him political information and advice suited to his needs and his view of the political world.[3]

4. If we could imagine a "beginning" of such a process of interchange, the communications moving upward on the ladder would be no more than expressions of general discontent and vague aspiration. For certainly the uninformed citizen would not have well-formulated policy preferences to communicate upward.

5. But it follows from what has already been said that the upward flow of opinion is a good deal more than the expression of vague aspiration and discontent. It is a more specific statement of discontent, aspiration, and policy preference profiting from the downward flow and undergoing increasing refinement as it moves upward. The quality of the upward flow is improved both by the improved competence of those below, and by the tendency of many of those below to delegate to their more competent associates, or to participants at a higher level. We know that some citizens do not vote, delegating to other voters; that some voters do not vote according to policy preferences, leaving it to others to do so; that all voters leave most specific policy issues to proximate policy makers to decide; and that congressmen delegate on some issues to the President, and on some issues to their better-informed colleagues.

6. At some levels the described interchange of influence is supplemented by other patterns. Specifically, some *upward* communication is from the more informed to the less informed, as in the case of interest-group use of partisan analysis to persuade various kinds of proximate policy makers.

7. The upward flow of communication and other influence is stronger from persons and groups who can afford the high costs of, or themselves practice, the skills of political persuasion, and weaker from those who cannot. It is at its weakest in the case of persons who are poor, poorly educated, and without minimum political and organizational skills.

8. The process of two-way influence is fundamental and comprehensive in democratic systems. Proximate policy makers are engaged in it for most of their waking hours. Citizens participate in it whenever they express a political prefer-

[3] Because at each lower step participants want the higher step to offer analysis and advice suited to their general dispositions, and because at each higher step participants compete for followings at lower steps, most communication will take place between participants who have some important values or views in common. A citizen will listen more often and more attentively to an interest-group leader who in some important sense agrees with him than to one who does not. This accounts in part for what superficially appears to be a paradox—that discussion on political issues is largely between those who already agree—noted in V. O. Key, Jr., *Public Opinion and American Democracy* (New York: Alfred A. Knopf, 1961), p. 354; and R. B. Berelson, P. F. Lazarsfeld, and W. N. McPhee, *Voting* (Chicago: University of Chicago Press, 1954), p. 106.

Reconstructing Preferences

ence, whenever they read editorial comments in their newspapers, whenever they give their attention to any low- or high-level public opinion leader. Even some non-voting, apathetic citizens will occasionally rise to a vote or other expression of discontent—or by their inactivity signal upward that the policy-making process is working well enough not to trigger their active participation in it.

The process reaches deeply into the life of most ordinary citizens, even to those who pick up almost no political information or advice from officials or candidates, or from newspapers, magazines, radio, or television. For we have seen that at the very bottom of the ladder the more active and informed citizen informally communicates with the near-apathetic. Opinion leadership of this kind serves to upgrade the quality of citizen participation, serves to articulate the needs of some of the least articulate members of the political community and keep them in touch with communications flowing down from above.[4] Nevertheless, the process is not all-pervasive, at least not vigorously so, for there are some large groups—many Negroes both north and south, and Mexicans in the southwest states, for example—who are hardly linked into the interchange.

9. The process pushes participants toward agreement because preferences are re-formed by information about what is possible and feasible and because, as we have seen, the most active participants recognize the need for agreement.

10. The agreement achieved is not simply an agreement that suits the private preferences of those higher up on the ladder, for at most levels, as we have already noted, those above must compete for followings among those below.

11. The alterations of preferences in the direction of agreement include alterations that are comprehensive and fundamental. Although it is difficult to isolate so diffuse a social process for empirical testing of its results, it seems reasonable to believe that the degree of political consensus achieved in well-developed democratic political systems and markedly less well achieved in, say, most of the Latin-American regimes, is in large part a consequence of the strength of this two-way process in the developed democracies. Thus even the basic consensus that is often alleged to make democratic policy making possible is perhaps in fact itself a product of the policy-making process.[5]

Reconstructive Leadership

It follows from our discussion of the policy-making ladder that at any given time, proximate policy makers have to make their policy decisions within the constraints of existing preferences (of citizens and leaders). Over time, however, they have many opportunities to alter the preferences that at any given time constrain them.

A leader who sees this possibility and who is skilled enough to exploit it we shall call a reconstructive leader. He neither resigns himself to the constraint of preferences as he finds them, nor, on the other hand, does he necessarily attempt the impossible task of winning all other participants over to his views or preferences. He takes the middle course of shifting others' preferences so that the policies he desires fall within (whereas they formerly fell outside) the constraints imposed by the preferences of other participants in policy making. And he then uses what power or influence he has to get the policy he wants.

[4] For evidence on how far down the ladder reaches, see Key, *Public Opinion and American Democracy*, p. 361; and R. E. Lane, *Political Life* (Glencoe, Ill.: The Free Press, 1959), p. 91.

[5] On sources of consensus, see Key, *Public Opinion and American Democracy*, Ch. 2.

What is the significance of reconstructive leadership? In the first place, simply to identify the possibility of it is to correct a tendency in some contemporary political science to underplay the role of high-level leadership in democratic policy making.

In some schools of thought, it is either argued or implicitly assumed that the pressure of existing interests or preferences, especially segmental or group interests, imprisons the would-be leader.[6] If one assumes that to achieve a significant impact on policy an ambitious leader has to win a large number of other participants in policy making over to his own views or preferences, it does indeed look as though significant leadership in contemporary pluralist democracies, in which all kinds of preferences of all kinds of groups impose themselves on policy, is an impossibility. When, however, leadership attempts not to win support for its preferences but instead to win no more than a shift in the structure of preferences so that it can then move in the play of power to policies earlier outside the range of the possible, leadership is possible.

We can cite many examples. Realizing that, given the distribution of attitudes in the late 1930's, entering the war on the side of the Allies was out of the question, President Franklin Roosevelt set about shifting these attitudes. And even many lesser politicians seem to take for granted that the function of leadership is to reconstruct interests in order to give themselves new scope for policy making. Witness the efforts of President Johnson, especially in his first presidential campaign, to achieve a new political consensus. De Gaulle is another example: After coming back into power in 1958 to cope with the Algerian crisis, he appears not to have tried to mold political preferences to agree with his policies, but only to shift them enough so that his policies would emerge from the inevitable compromise of interests inherent in the French system.

RECONSTRUCTION VERSUS COMPROMISE

Reconstructive leadership is significant, secondly, because it is an alternative to leadership of another kind: the simple compromise of unreconstructed preferences. We often admire the skills of the compromiser. Henry Clay, for example, has gone down in American history as "the great compromiser." On Nehru's death, Shastri's popularity as a candidate for the succession stemmed from his skill in political compromise. Yet compromise of existing preferences or interests is often dangerous. Clay's compromises achieved little in avoiding the Civil War; and Shastri, though keeping the political peace within India, did not achieve the new directions in policy that were urgently needed for Indian development. What every modern political system requires is *moving* compromise—specifically, a never-ending sequence of compromises, each successive one responding to a new alignment of preferences or interests. Leadership that understands this fact, and that molds the moving structure of preferences, opens up significant new departures in policy, as Franklin Roosevelt did and as Shastri did not.

[6] It seems implicit, for example, in E. Latham, *The Group Basis of Politics* (Ithaca: Cornell University Press, 1952), Ch. 1.

Reconstructing Preferences

Some
Clouded
Views

How now to complete an overview of the policy-making process as a whole?[1]
A device that lends itself to the purpose is to consider three
currently popular allegations about how the American policy-making
system "really" works. The first is that the system is out of control,
not responsive to anyone in any rational way. The second
is that it is actually controlled by an elite.

[1] For a summary of the entire analysis up to this point, see
the appendix at the end of this chapter.

And the third is that, whether dominated by an elite or by a heterogeneous collection of political leaders, interest groups, and unusually influential citizens, it is not sufficiently responsive to ordinary citizens. We shall take up each allegation in turn.

No Rational Control?

Some people see policy making as under no one's rational control because policies emerge from a confused interplay in which no one takes responsibility for, and no one can be specifically identified as author of, a policy choice. An appropriations bill is signed into law. Congressmen disclaim responsibility; they say they were compelled to go along with the President's budget. The President disclaims responsibility, saying that Congress can, and did, do as it pleased. Or House members claim the bill is really the Senate's, senators simultaneously claiming that the Senate merely followed House leadership. And no one is clear whether the House action was dominated by the Rules Committee, by an appropriations sub-committee, by the Chairman of the Appropriations Committee, or by some other leader or group.

It would be a mistake to take any of this as unambiguous evidence of irrationality. For in any complex cooperative process with widespread participation, the outcome is necessarily a joint product of the interactions of all participants. If that makes analysis of the causes or origins of a policy discouragingly difficult, the difficulty is not to be confused with irrationality in the complex process itself.

Still it does seem at times that policy making is conspicuously incompetent. Government appears to embark on wars that nobody wants, falls down on such elementary tasks as maintaining law and order in our big cities, and simply fails—as though paralyzed—to respond to demands for rapid significant improvement in the social condition of the urban poor.

Policy making, however, is what it is because participants in the policy-making process behave as they do. Men make policy; it is not made for them. They also make the policy-making machinery. Much of what might be called the "irrationality" of the policy-making system is, therefore, the consequence of the irrationality of the participants in it. It may be serious—even disastrous. But it represents the quality of man's control over policy making, not the absence of it.

But is the system sometimes irrational even when participants in it are not? What kinds of *system* irrationalities might we find? Pressure in the system to turn out policy decisions with insufficient deliberation? Inconsistency? Apparent failure to choose policies appropriate to ends in view. It turns out, again, that none of these necessarily proves irrationality. Let us see why this is so.

MISLEADING EVIDENCE

Irrationality as hurried and uninformed decision making? One can ask how much thought and study go into policy making—and indeed we have looked at length, especially in our early chapters, into this question. But such a concept of irrationality does not carry us far in appraising policy making, since all policy-making systems will, for all the reasons we have seen, not go very far toward thoughtful and informed decisions. Nor do we really

108

think it would improve policy making if, as a universal rule, thought and study were pushed further, for study and thinking are expensive and time-consuming. It would be irrational to push dispassionate analysis to its outer limits, in the meantime holding up all decisions. Policy making at its best has to cope quickly with problems, finding solutions before all the facts are in, and doing so by giving policy-making tasks to the less-than-ideally-competent people who inhabit the earth.

Irrationality as inconsistency in policy making? Though some forms of inconsistency are irrational, many are not. Because policy makers learn through trial and error, we should not ask that today's policy be consistent with yesterday's. Because policy makers learn through trial and error about goals as well as means, we should not ask even that policies not waver or alter in their objectives; we should hope instead that they do. Because in a pluralist, complex society, social goals are not a tightly knit harmonious structure, because we value openness in goal structure, and because we keep the social peace by permitting conflicting groups to pursue conflicting goals, we do not even want to reject such apparent inconsistencies as—to take a common example—subsidizing some farmers to restrict output, and others to expand it. Depending on who the farmers are, what their crops are, where their land is, and how subsidies affect them, both subsidies may make sense.

Irrationality as maladaptation of means to an end? Even this respectable concept of irrationality is inapplicable because of disagreement on ends among participants in policy making. If they disagree, how can we say whether the means they decide on do or do not suit the ends? Whatever policies are decided on will ordinarily suit some group's ends or goals. But it will also be true that they will not suit another group's goals, and can always therefore be condemned as irrational.

Moreover, because in the play of power a cluster of means has to be adapted to a cluster of ends, it again becomes impossible to say whether means suit ends or not. Suppose a congressman wants:

desegregation in transport	to improve conditions of Negroes
aid to Pakistan	to develop Pakistan
a tax cut	to increase consumer spending
forestation	to curtail soil erosion

He may, in informal mutual adjustment with his colleagues, give up on aid to Pakistan in order to hold fast on the tax cut, or trade his influence on forestation to gain some influence on desegregation. Looking at the outcome, we find him voting against forestation and aid to Pakistan, despite his genuine desire both to curtail soil erosion and to develop Pakistan. We cannot say that his turning against the means suitable to some of his ends is irrational, nor can we actually say that, taking all his ends as a group, he did not choose the correct means.

NO ADEQUATE CRITERIA

Out of the policy-making system come terrible mistakes—and even oftener come policies that you, I, or someone else deplores. To say, however, that a policy was irrationally chosen would require, it now becomes clear, an investigation of all the circumstances of the choice, including the time pressure 109 under which it had to be made, the state of knowledge concerning it, the need for delegation, the appropriate methods of cooperation, the possibility of partisan analysis of the issues, the relation of the choice to other interlocked policy choices, the extent of disagreement on goals—in fact, of all the aspects of policy making discussed in this book. And even with such a wide-ranging investigation, one will usually come up with disputed conclusions as to whether the choice was or was not well made and whether it could have been made better. For we do not quite know which characteristics of policy making we should call rational. (Just how studied should a decision be? When should decisions be consistent and when not?) In the present state of social science, a concept of rationality appropriate for judging a complex political system cannot be defined.[2]

A Ruling Elite?

The second allegation—that an elite dominates American policy making—is a slippery one to pin down for analysis. Depending on how one uses words, there is or is not a dominant elite. No group gets its way all the time on every issue. On the other hand, some groups and kinds of participants in the play of power are obviously more powerful than others.

An official elite? As we have seen, proximate policy making is the task of a relatively small group of officials and other political leaders. Any one official exerts enormously more effect on policy than any single ordinary citizen. Bearing in mind what proximate policy makers can and cannot do (the discretion they enjoy in policy making), one might say that they "dominate" policy making. If so, proximate policy makers are the ruling elite.

Such a conclusion is neither new nor interesting; it is only a colorfully imprecise way of characterizing an aspect of policy making described more precisely in the preceding chapters.

Interest-group elites? Aside from the proximate policy makers, interest-group leaders are conspicuously influential in policy making. Sometimes officials hold them at arm's length; but sometimes, we have seen, interest-group leaders establish a confidential relationship, with the result that on some issues the official simply does what they advise. For example, the corporate laws of at least 15 states were written largely by a committee of the American Bar Association. On some issues, the Bar will be powerful; on others, the American Medical Association; on others, the AFL-CIO; and so on. One might say, therefore, that groups consisting of officials associated with interest-group leaders constitute a collection of elites, each with dominant influence in its particular field. But, again, this introduces nothing new into our analysis, and it refers roughly and imprecisely to processes already described more precisely.[3]

[2] For clarifying discussion on the meaning of rationality in its broadest sense, see K. Mannheim, *Man and Society in An Age of Reconstruction* (New York: Harcourt, Brace and Co., 1948), pp. 51–60; on citizen rationality, see R. E. Lane and D. O. Sears, *Public Opinion*, Foundations of Modern Political Science Series (Englewood Cliffs, N. J.: Prentice-Hall, Inc., 1964), Ch. 7; and on administrative rationality, H. A. Simon, *Administrative Behavior*, 2nd ed. (New York: The Macmillan Company, 1959), Ch. 4.

[3] Both kinds of "elite"—the proximate policy makers and the associated groups of officials and interest-group leaders—are drawn from among the best-educated members of

Some Clouded Views

An Establishment elite? In the idea of the Establishment[4] is to be found a core of an important perception about policy making. Given the role that policy analysis plays in policy making and in the all-pervasive power of partisan analysis, those who can analyze skillfully do indeed achieve great influence. Men who can bring relevant fact and analysis to bear on a political issue can, without holding office or heading an interest group, achieve influence disproportionate to their numbers. And they have come to be increasingly conspicuous as the demand for analysis multiplies with the technical complexity of policy making in the modern world. In a field like international relations, for example, the hundreds of informal conferences arranged by the Council on Foreign Relations, and the pages of its journal, *Foreign Affairs,* constitute forums in which all kinds of *men who know* from government, private associations, universities, and newspapers talk about public policy with great effect on the proximate policy makers who are among them.

Yet, again, to call the skilled practitioners of policy analysis an elite and to say that they "dominate" policy is to describe roughly and in colored terms a method of influence already described more precisely.

CONFLICTING ELITES

We saw in an earlier chapter that administrators occupy some of the key positions in the play of power. One might call them—some people do—a managerial elite. Because the wealthy exert, for reasons discussed in several earlier chapters, influence disproportionate to their numbers, we can call them an elite of wealth. Taking these groups together with those we have just discussed, we find—if we want to continue using the term—a variety of elites.

The variety itself, however, reduces the power of any one of them; and if we want to assess their influence as they conflict in the play of power, we have to go back into the kind of detailed analysis of participants and methods of interaction in the play of power that have occupied us throughout this book. We found no conspiracy that unites them all, and what we have seen of the play of power is evidence against any conspiracy beyond the arrangements for cooperation that are necessary in any policy-making system (and which, again, have been detailed in the preceding chapters). Again, therefore, to allege a governing elite is to say crudely what has been said more precisely.

There are those, however, who will simply disagree with the account, given in this book, of how policies are made. They allege that in some sense there is a homogeneous ruling elite that we have missed seeing. One of the strengths of this belief, to those who hold it, is that the methods of elite control are so subtle that they can hardly be disproved. Although a scattering of men both in public life and research repeatedly allege "a ruling elite," they

---

society. And because the best educated are drawn disproportionately from the wealthier segments of the population, they will disproportionately represent the well-off. Moreover, the largest source of finance for interest groups is the corporation; hence, interest groups will give, as we have already said, a "bias" to policy making. For these reasons, and for others that anyone can fill in more fully, the most active and immediate participants in policy making are a small group (relative to the size of the total population) of persons whose background, attitudes, and values are at best a skewed representation of the population as a whole. All this too we have seen in earlier chapters.

[4] First popularized in the U. S. by Richard Rovere's "The American Establishment," 57 *Esquire* (May, 1962).

Some Clouded Views

not only confuse the phenomenon of concentration of proximate policy making into the hands of a few with the existence of an elite, but also fail to document convincingly any disproportionate power other than what has been described in these chapters.[5]

The most significant efforts to find solid evidence have been through studies of community power—that is, of local government; and although a substantial dispute has developed over what sort of interpretation is to be put on their findings, those community studies that allege "a ruling elite" have not been able to weather criticism.[6] The controversy now is, roughly speaking, between those political scientists who are satisfied that a pluralist dispersal of influence rather than an elitist concentration is inevitable in American politics, and those who wish to consider further the possibility of indirect and less tangible elitist influences on local government.[7]

Some people think they see the work of a homogeneous elite in American history: in the nineteenth and early twentieth century bitter resistance to trade unions; in the slowness with which social security legislation appeared on the books; in continuing timidity on public medical care programs; in extraordinary freedom given business enterprise; in antagonism to concepts and forms of socialism acceptable in other democratic countries; and of course in the continued (though declining) harshness of whites to Negroes.

To explain such phenomena as these in elitist terms seems both unnecessary and imprecise. In some large part, these policies and resistances represent the influence on policy of an overwhelming majority of citizens—for an overwhelming majority did in fact once oppose trade unions, did in fact once believe in a wide scope of freedom for business, and does in fact still wish to discriminate between Negroes and whites. Moreover, insofar as policies and resistances of this kind can be explained as the product of minority wishes, they can be explained as the product of the kinds of biases discussed in some detail in earlier chapters. Finally, it is clear from the list of examples that no one homogeneous elite could possibly account for them. One has to distinguish between the white elite that oppresses Negroes, and the professional elite that has carried the fight against health insurance. But, then again, if any group or category of policy makers that exerts power disproportionate to its size is to be called an elite, we hardly need the term.

DEMOCRATIC NORMS

Elitist allegations often respond to an inappropriate desire to answer the question, "Who makes policy?"—a question that we saw in Chapter Five to

[5] For an example, see C. W. Mills, *The Power Elite* (New York: Oxford University Press, 1956), and a long, careful review by Talcott Parsons, 10 *World Politics* (October, 1957), pp. 123–143, that comments on Mills' lack of evidence, as well as on analytical errors. See also the references to elitist writers in Chapter Five above. More insightful older elitist theory is in Vilfredo Pareto, *The Mind and Society* (1916) (New York: Harcourt, Brace, 1935); Gaetano Mosca, *The Ruling Class* (1896) (New York: McGraw-Hill, 1939); and Robert Michels, *Political Parties* (1911) (Glencoe, Ill.: The Free Press, 1949).

[6] For example, F. Hunter, *Community Power Structure* (Chapel Hill, N. C.: University of North Carolina Press, 1953); and appraisal of it and other community power studies in N. W. Polsby, *Community Power and Political Theory* (New Haven: Yale University Press, 1963).

[7] P. Bachrach and M. S. Baratz, "Decisions and Non-Decisions," 57 *American Political Science Review* (September, 1963).

Some Clouded Views

be less pertinent than the question, "What makes policy?" For policy making is a complicated cooperative process that cannot be described by pointing a finger at a "who." If it is granted that policy making is an intricate cooperative process in which a variety of elites (if one insists on the term) participates, a better question to ask than the clumsy "Is there an elite?" is whether the powers of the various "elites" we have considered are reasonably consistent with democratic aspirations.

Such a question is, for the time being, largely unanswerable, but it serves to identify a field of political theory that needs developing. What is a "democratic" relationship between elected and appointed officials? Between interest-group leaders and officials? Between men skilled in policy analysis and proximate policy makers? Democratic theory has been so occupied with laying down the definitive features of elections and party competition in a democracy that it has badly neglected the attempt to develop criteria for democracy in the complex interactions of the most active policy makers. If some possible patterns of interrelationship among them are clearly undemocratic, as in the Soviet Union, many of the patterns we have found in so-called democratic regimes—like the frequent close relationship between official and interest group—need a good deal more thinking out.

A quick way to come to an adverse conclusion on the question of consistency between democratic aspirations and the roles of the most active is to take the position that, in any case, democratic aspirations require more active citizen participation to reduce "elite" powers. But how much more? If, as is plain, not everyone can be a proximate policy maker, just how much and what kind of citizen participation is required to achieve democratic aspirations? For those whose idea of democracy is the New England town meeting of earlier years, or a meeting of citizens of Athens, what is required is far more than is possible. On the other hand, concepts of democracy adapted to modern, large-scale systems, in which proximate policy making is delegated to a small group, do not adequately spell out the desired role for the citizen, except for identifying such obvious flaws in democracy as the exclusion of some citizens from the system.[8] Hence, simply for lack of insight on what democratic aspirations are or ought to be, we cannot say whether the American policy-making system lives up to them or not.

Could we fall back on the idea that, whatever else we do not know, majority rule is necessary to democratic aspirations, and ask whether the role of "elites" is consistent with majority rule? Not very well. In the immediate or proximate sense, the majority cannot rule; they delegate rule to proximate policy makers. Is it necessary to democracy that the proximate policy makers be held to those policies that win majority assent? We have seen that on many policy questions most citizens do not have opinions—and do not want to have to form them. Should democratic proximate policy makers hold to policies that would suit a majority of citizens if citizens did hold an opinion? Not necessarily, for we have seen that citizens and proximate policy makers alike know that on many issues a citizen opinion, if formed, would be incompetent.

[8] For some controversy about the differences in the concepts and their implications for citizen participation, see J. L. Walker, "A Critique of Elitist Theories of Democracy," and a reply by R. A. Dahl, both in 60 *American Political Science Review* (June, 1966).

Some Clouded Views

In a democracy, citizens do not necessarily want policy to follow hypothetical majority opinions or preferences; they want to delegate to some kind of "elite."[9]

Does the Ordinary Citizen Really Count?

In the meantime, regardless of democratic aspirations, many informed and thoughtful citizens, as well as educated young people approaching voting age, complain that the policy-making system is simply too big, too cumbersome for them to move. They are roughly correct, given what they are willing to do about it. Any single citizen is only one of millions. Taken by himself as an ordinary citizen, he is almost powerless. The complaint is best brought, however, against the number of people in the system, not against the design of the system. For no ordinary citizen among many millions can by himself be powerful in policy making. For that matter, would anyone want him to be? How much power can be given to each one among many millions?

If, however, the size of the system belittles the power of the ordinary citizen, the design of the system permits him, if he wishes and under some circumstances, to exert considerable influence. The system permits those who wish to do so to gain back some of what mere numbers take away.

First, we have seen that, in a democratic system, party competition gives most inactive citizens a voice in policy making, simply because competing parties are concerned about citizen preferences.

Second, we have seen that a democratic policy-making system parcels out the tasks of policy making between ordinary citizens and proximate policy makers so that most ordinary citizens who wish to do so can join in voting to choose the proximate policy makers.

Third, it so divides up the tasks of policy making that, whatever a competent citizen's energies or particular interests, there is likely to be a task or role suited to him: interest-group work, party work, running for office, and the like.

In short, although most citizens influence policy only a little, extremely energetic citizens with some competence can influence it very much.

ARE SOME CITIZENS POWERLESS?

Does this mean that no one need be powerless in a democratic system? Drawing on several of the preceding chapters, we can see that a combination of circumstances can indeed render a citizen powerless, for reasons other than his own quite voluntary refusal to participate in policy making. The combination is: poverty, poor education, social isolation from other participants, and inadequate political socialization.

Poverty obstructs participation because, as we have seen, many forms of

[9] Moreover, we have seen that there are various kinds of majorities. A majority can be built up around policies of widely shared benefits. Or around a cluster of policies, each of which offers something to some minority, so that the cluster as a whole appeals to a majority. Policies can appeal to a majority of citizens, a majority of voters, or a majority of those active enough to make their views on policy explicit. Or a majority can be a more-or-less permanent one, as in a system with disciplined parties, or a majority constantly forming and reforming around each new issue, as tends to be the case in American politics. Which of all these possible majorities should rule in a democracy? Perhaps one on some issues, another on others? But, if so, then, again, we cannot, what with the present state of democratic theory, say much about what "elites" should and should not be able to do.

Some Clouded Views

political persuasion are expensive, and some forms of participation require leisure time.

Poor education obstructs because, in more circumstances than not, one gets the policies he wants, as we have seen, not simply by asserting a demand but by giving reasons—specifically, by skill in analysis. A sufficiently poor education leaves political issues, and the design of strategies to achieve influence, hopelessly beyond the competence of the citizen.

Social isolation of an individual or a group, we have seen, renders impossible the construction of alliances necessary to achieve influence, and even throws roadblocks in the way of acquiring the most elementary necessary political information and skill through informal interchange.

Inadequate socialization, we have seen, renders citizens powerless in ways that look like voluntary withdrawal. Most citizens are appropriately socialized.[10] They pick up from family, school, friends, clubs, and political parties the attitudes and dispositions to action that lead them habitually to vote and to organize politically. At least some of the members of various economic, ethnic, regional, and other groups pick up elementary skills in organization and communication. And, people pick up both aspirations great enough to motivate them, and expectations not so bleak as to discourage them.

A citizen who has not been socialized in any of these ways will not vote or otherwise participate in policy making. Even if he suffers from ills from which he knows appropriate policies could protect him, and even if he would like to do something positive about his problems, he will not see in voting or other participation any practical, realizable possibility for helping himself (and, incidentally, he will be as rational in his view as the socialized citizen).

Are there people who suffer from such a combination of barriers to participation in policy making? Of immigrants to the U. S., millions have so suffered—either temporarily or for their lifetimes in America. Today the largest group by far is, of course, the Negro, of whom millions are poor, uneducated, cut off from white citizens (as well as from well-off, educated Negroes), and without habits, aspirations, or expectations that would support participation, and without any skills in organization and communication.[11]

WHAT THE CITIZEN MUST BE, HAVE, AND DO TO INFLUENCE POLICY

And so we refine the earlier statement. Even in a democracy, not every citizen can influence policy. Only those can who have some reason to think it matters, who possess the skills and resources of citizenship, whose aspirations and expectations are stimulating rather than paralyzing, and who are—and *feel* they are—members of the political community. But even in that group some will feel thwarted at their inability to achieve a perceptible influence on policy. For something else is required, too: work. Policy making is laborious; there is no escaping its burdens. For other than scholars, philosophers, and publicists whose ideas are powerful enough to influence policy at a distance (and even they have to work at the formulation and communication of their ideas), a big share in policy making is reserved to those who look at participation in the play of power not as a privilege but as a task, job, or career.

[10] G. A. Almond and G. B. Powell, Jr., *Comparative Politics* (Boston: Little, Brown & Co., 1966), Ch. 3.

[11] And perhaps a million and a half are simply not allowed to vote. Even if the law says they can, informal extra-legal rules are enforced to prohibit them from doing it.

Some Clouded Views

Appendix: Summary of Analysis

Analytic Policy Making

Inventive as man has been in extending his analytical capacities, he cannot follow through to a conclusive analysis of the merits of alternative policies. Policy problems simply run beyond his analytical competence. In particular, the merits of many of the goals or values that men contemplate pursuing through public policy cannot be empirically verified as can beliefs about facts, but are instead subject to endless dispute. Then, too, many citizens and leaders simply distrust analysis and analysts.

The Play of Power

"Power" to decide. How then can men decide on policy? Some person or persons must simply make policy choices for the society, the rest of the population simply accepting the decisions. The policy-making task or function has to be seized or assigned.

Whoever takes on the task will of course employ analysis up to a point. He must, however, come to a decision—by guess, considered judgment, or whim.

The task or responsibility cannot be laid upon one man or small group. Even an authoritarian ruler needs a structure of subordinate colleagues to assist him in policy making. In the democracies, almost every adult is offered a share of the task, and many accept. For example—though examples do not do justice to the complexities of task definition and assignment—some (President, Prime Minister, or Cabinet) accept the principal responsibility for initiating policy decisions; others the (legislative) task of amending, ratifying, or rejecting these policy initiatives; others the (judicial) task of testing policy decisions for consistency with constitutional rules; and others, the task of deciding who will be a member, say, of the legislative group—a task they are able to discharge through voting.

Rules and authority. Such a process—both the relatively simpler one of authoritarian policy making and the intricate one of democratic policy making—works because somehow people perform the tasks they accept, and others accept the results. But why do people accept? They may be terrorized into so doing by someone or some group that can command a personal guard, police force, or army. In democratic societies, however, they do so for a variety of other reasons. Some people like the tasks that have been assigned, or the money, prestige, and sense of power that go with them. Others who like to be left free of responsibility are willing to accept what is decided upon. Some people simply believe that, since some assignment of tasks is necessary, they ought morally to perform their assigned task and go along with others who perform theirs. Others perform their tasks, or accept the results of those who do, because they fear the enmity of their neighbors and associates if they fail to do so, or because those who do accept their assignments have organized routines for fining, jailing, or otherwise punishing others.

Whatever the reasons, most people adopt a *rule* of performing an accepted task according to the task's specifications, and a *rule* of accepting the decisions of those to whom tasks have been assigned. They do not ask themselves at every opportunity: "Could I get away with defaulting?" Some of the rules they accept are those of obedience on specified matters to specified categories of persons, thus establishing the *authority* of those persons.

116

Specialization. A proliferation of specialized tasks in policy making arises both as a method of raising the competence of policy makers (since no one participant in the process can be competent in all areas and on all aspects of policy making) and as a method of limiting the power or influence of any one policy maker. In democratic societies, an especially intricate specialization of function—carried to an extreme in the American pattern of checks and balances—greatly constrains the power or influence of any one policy maker.

Cooperation. Hence in all policy-making systems, but especially in democratic systems, policies can be made only through the cooperation of many participants, each of whom performs a task that is necessary, but itself insufficient, to establish a policy decision. Policy making is a cooperative collective effort, and policy a joint output, beyond the capacity of any one person or any small group of those to whom policy-making tasks are assigned.

Proximate policy makers in the key roles. Two forms of specialization of task are especially important for determining the character of the cooperative process. One is specialization of the immediate, or proximate, responsibility to a small fraction of the adult population and (in a democracy) to a small fraction of the total number of people to whom policy-making tasks are assigned. Most policy makers in a democracy have the lightest of tasks—and even those only at their own option: voting, interest-group membership, communications to the proximate policy makers, and the like.

The other form of specialization of task is detailed specialization within the proximate policy-making group. In American national government, for example, significant specializations, among others, are President, Supreme Court justices, appellate court justices, majority and minority party leader in each House, congressional committee chairmen, Speaker of the House, and bureau chiefs.

Cooperation among proximate policy makers. The proximate policy makers, each performing his specialized task, find it possible to cooperate—that is, jointly to arrive at policy decisions—because: (1) they are constrained and instructed not only by the general rules that hold for all participants, but by special rules holding for proximate policy makers alone; (2) they use their authority over each other directly and indirectly; and (3) they both persuade each other and reconsider their own policy positions.

Organized and informal cooperation. To facilitate their cooperation, they both establish formal organizations like congressional committees and parties (thus creating a government within government) and practice a variety of informal techniques of mutual adjustment.

NEW SCOPE FOR (A REVISED FORM OF) POLICY ANALYSIS

In their attempt to persuade others to cooperate or to find a more cooperative policy position for themselves, proximate policy makers and other leaders turn policy analysis into a fundamental tactic in the play of power. In their hands, policy analysis is no longer an alternative to a play of power; it becomes largely an instrument of influence or power. It becomes a way of fighting over policy.

Policy is analyzed not in an unrealistic attempt to reach conclusive determinations of correct policy, but simply to persuade. And it does not run afoul of disagreement on goals or values, as does the kind of analysis discussed in the early chapters, because it accepts as generally valid the values of the policy maker to whom it is addressed.

THE OTHER PARTICIPANTS

Interest-group leaders. Interest-group leaders are an important category of unusually active participants in the policy-making process who, with some excep-

Appendix: Summary of Analysis

tions, are without legal or extra-legal authority to make proximate decisions on policy. They are therefore heavily dependent on the other major method of exerting power or influence: persuasion through the practice of partisan analysis. So diligent and skilled are many of them that they become powerful indeed. They come to serve as major sources of information and analysis for those proximate policy makers who do have authority.

The ordinary citizen. Ordinary citizens, however, play a relatively inactive role in policy making. They very largely delegate or yield the resolution of policy questions to proximate policy makers, though sometimes intervening to hold these policy makers to a desired position. It is generally difficult for either a candidate or an interest-group leader to mobilize the citizens' votes around specific issues; it can only be done on a few issues of unusual concern to citizens. In the democracies citizens do, however, choose the top proximate policy makers (who are, at the same time, those who appoint the other proximate policy makers), a task that indirectly gives them substantially more leverage on policy making than they actively pursue, because of the peculiar role played by political parties.

Parties and elections. Competition for office, organized and intensified by clustering of candidates into political parties, drives the parties and their candidates into a study of what the citizen wants, although parties try to attract votes by mere rhetoric and by irrational and nonrational appeals, as well as by taking policy positions that they believe, on investigation, to correspond to what the voter wants. The effect of party competition is—to a degree—to make proximate policy makers more responsive to demands or preferences of relatively passive citizens than would be the case if citizens had to "signal" their wishes, with some positive action on their part, to the proximate policy makers.

Reconstruction of Preferences

The policy-making ladder. But parties, proximate policy makers, interest-group leaders, and other leaders, do not simply respond to citizen preferences; in various ways they inform, persuade, and indoctrinate the citizen. The policy-making process, therefore, becomes circular. It can also be conceived of as a ladder with chief executive on top, ordinary citizens at the bottom, and other participants ranged on the intermediate rungs. Citizens send *upward* their opinions and preferences; but at each rung of the ladder a more informed, active, or responsible participant in policy making is sending *downward* some information, analysis, and advice that help a participant on a lower rung to clarify and amend his policy position, and that eventually reach down to help citizens understand and better express their own wishes and needs.

Reconstructive leadership. It follows that there is great scope in policy making for political leaders who appreciate the possibilities of reconstructing the preferences both of citizens and of other participants in policy making, and who skillfully alter the position of the range of alternatives within which policy decisions must fall.

Appendix: Summary of Analysis

To Explore Further

Looking back at the range of topics embraced in this book, it is not clear what further reading would *not* be appropriate to enrich one's understanding of policy making. We have discussed a wide range of topics: how men analyze problems; their specialized devices for problem solving; methods for manufacturing and disseminating information; the character of public discussion on public problems; law and other methods of rule making; how men influence each other; specific institutions like the presidency and congressional committees; the public interest; utility theory; the "war of all against all"; and so on.

Most of the suggested readings that might appear here have therefore been listed in footnotes so placed as to indicate with some precision which topics they further develop. What to read further on any specified topic that we have discussed can often be found by referring back to that topic through the table of contents or index.

Convenient sources, of course, for further reading on a number of the larger aspects of policy making are other books so far published in this series. On citizen behavior and the formation of public opinion: R. E. Lane and D. O. Sears, *Public Opinion* (Englewood Cliffs, N. J.: Prentice-Hall, Inc., 1964). On voting and parties: F. I. Greenstein, *The American Party System and the American People* (Englewood Cliffs, N. J.: Prentice-Hall, Inc., 1963). On the proximate policy makers: N. W. Polsby, *Congress and the Presidency* (Englewood Cliffs, N. J.: Prentice-Hall, Inc., 1964). On local government, which we have slighted, and for more on state government: H. Kaufman, *Politics and Policies in State and Local Governments* (Englewood Cliffs, N. J.: Prentice-Hall, Inc., 1964). Each book in this series contains an annotated bibliography.

Because the policy-making process is not a well-defined, established field in political science, it is not possible to refer to books that stand squarely and explicitly in the middle of it. But I should like to single out for special attention four excellent works (three of which have been cited in the footnotes), each distinctly different from the other in method, and each of which analyzes with rare skill some large part of the policy-making process. D. B. Truman's *The Governmental Process* (New York: Alfred A. Knopf, 1960) is an empirically rich but at the same time theoretically explicit analysis of much of what we have embraced under policy making. S. H. Beer's *British Politics in the Collectivist Age* (New York: Alfred A. Knopf, 1966) illuminates some of the core contemporary policy-making processes by relating them to their historical antecedents. In *American Business and Public Policy* (New York: Atherton Press, 1963), a title that disguises the range of policy-making phenomena embraced in the book and underplays its significance, Raymond Bauer, Ithiel de Sola Pool, and Lewis Anthony Dexter have, as we have already said, achieved major new insights into the policy-making role of the legislator and his relations with interest-groups and constituents. A decade before the publication of Truman's book, Pendleton Herring laid out in *The Politics of Democracy* (New York: W. W. Norton, new edition, 1965) an extraordinarily insightful analysis of government, politics, and policy making, with a richer implicit than explicit theoretical content. Worth reading for itself as well as for the light it throws on the importance of Herring's work is a review of the new edition by Avery Leiserson in 60 *American Political Science Review* (June, 1966).

For another kind of reading, there are many available case studies of the work

119

of particular government agencies, of particular policy controversies, and of particular processes in government. Many of these can be read as—and some are intended to be—studies of the policy-making process. Among them are: A. Wildavsky, *Dixon-Yates: A Study in Power Politics* (New Haven: Yale University Press, 1962); E. Myerson and E. C. Banfield, *Politics, Planning, and the Public Interest: The Case of Public Housing in Chicago* (Glencoe, Ill.: The Free Press, 1955); A. F. Westin (ed.), *The Uses of Power: 7 Cases in American Politics* (New York: Harcourt, Brace & World, Inc., 1962); A. Maass, *Muddy Waters: The Army Engineers and the Nation's Rivers* (Cambridge, Mass.: Harvard University Press, 1951); A. L. Hirschman, *Journeys Toward Progress: Studies of Economic Policy-Making in Latin America* (New York: The Twentieth Century Fund, 1963); the chapter on the Council of Economic Advisers in H. L. Wilensky, *Organizational Intelligence: Knowledge and Policy in Government and Industry* (New York: Basic Books, Inc., 1967); and Polsby's chapter on the budgetary process, in his book cited above.

Some further reading might be designed to explore imaginatively the relationship between the particular social processes represented in this book and certain others to which they might bear an especially interesting relationship. For an example, one's perceptions of the process of governmental policy making might be sharpened by seeing it set beside another quite different "policy-making" process. In *Politics, Economics and Welfare* (New York: Harper and Brothers, Publishers, 1953), R. A. Dahl and I have, to a degree, written a comparative study of policy making through the market system and policy making through government.

For another example, one might try to see the policy-making process in the light of the long-standing conflict between two sets of ideas of political problem-solving: the one stressing man's fallibility and the consequent need for liberal democratic political institutions; the other stressing man's competence, his potential for theoretical formulations sufficient to guide social reconstruction, and the consequent acceptability of authoritarian leadership in the hands of the competent. The two traditions are brilliantly discussed in J. L. Talmon, *The Origins of Totalitarian Democracy* (New York: Frederick A. Praeger, 1960).

Finally, as one more example, one might stretch his mind to see what can be extracted from some of the classics of political philosophy. It is stimulating to read, for example, Rousseau's *Social Contract,* to see how the concept of the General Will throws light on political socialization, consensus, and the role of analysis as an alternative to power—all taken as aspects of policy making.

To Explore Further